Human listening

PROCESSES AND BEHAVIOR

THE BOBBS-MERRILL SERIES IN *Speech Communication*

RUSSEL R. WINDES, *Editor*

Queens College of the City University of New York

CARL H. WEAVER

Ohio University

Human
listening

PROCESSES AND BEHAVIOR

Bobbs-Merrill Educational Publishing
Indianapolis

The Bobbs-Merrill Company, Inc.
4300 West 62nd Street
Indianapolis, Indiana 46268

Fourth Printing 1976
Library of Congress Catalog Card Number: 75-182878
ISBN: 0-672-61234-8 (pbk)

Editor's foreword

The conversation between an experienced psychiatrist and a young M.D. just finishing his residency in psychiatry has become a classic anecdote. "I don't know how you have done it all these years," the young M.D. said, "six or eight hours a day, five days a week, forty-eight weeks a year, for twenty-five years—listening, listening, listening—constantly listening to other people's problems. How have you been able to listen all this time?" The older psychiatrist thought a few seconds and then said, "Who listens?"

"Who listens?" is a universal complaint. Parents don't listen to children. Children don't listen to parents. Students don't listen to teachers, and teachers don't listen to students. Voters and politicians don't listen to one another. The Russians don't listen to the Chinese who don't listen to the Americans, who don't listen to the emerging nations, and so it goes. In many ways we have developed the art of speaking and writing, that is, expressing our own ideas to others, and almost ignored the companion arts of listening and reading. We presume that **to talk** is **to communicate,** or **to write** is **to communicate.** In fact, communication is a process which includes a message, a sender, and a **receiver,** and, in most cases, a response by the receiver to both the message and the sender. Yet alleged communication is often more or less a game between speaker and auditor; the speaker assumes he is being listened to; the auditor gives the impression that he is, indeed, listening and reacting, even though he may have, for the most part, tuned out the speaker. The game may be, from time to time, fun to play, but often the results are tragic. Information and judgments which are badly needed by the listener are never actually communicated.

We should not jump to the conclusion that everyone needs to listen constantly and seriously to everyone else. To do this would not only be a regrettable waste of time, but it would unquestionably transform all of us into obsessive and neurotic "inputers." But there are altogether too many occasions in daily living when so much is riding on our ability to hear, to listen to what we hear, and to perceive correctly what we listen to—the needs of a loved one, the instructions of an authority, the caveats of a knowledgeable and concerned friend. How many accidents could be prevented if we could train children to listen carefully? How many traumas might we be saved if we could train ourselves to listen carefully? How many of the despairs and frustrations of the technetronic age might we avoid, or at least condition ourselves to endure, if we attempted to balance our "output" of information and feelings with our "input"?

If listening is as vital to our survival and our sanity as talking, why don't we teach our youngsters from earliest childhood about listening and how to listen? Part of the answer is that we have generally failed to acknowledge the importance of listening. Moreover, even recognizing the importance of this subject, we have too frequently shrugged our shoulders as if to say, "There's no way to teach or learn listening." In effect, we have said that listening is **not** a behavior which can be modified. In another volume in the Bobbs-Merrill Series in Speech Communication **(Audience Analysis)** Professor Clevenger addressed himself to this problem:

> Any analysis of individual auditors must begin with the recognition that listening is behavior. It is an ancient and obvious truism—but one often overlooked—that listening is not a passive activity. Even the most relaxed and effortless sort of listening . . . involves doing something. In certain instances, superficial analysis may give the impression that the listener . . . is in reality a "passive" instrument in the hands of a skilled communicator who activates desired responses in the listener

by administering the correct sequence of stimuli. However, more de-
tailed examination reveals a very different picture, one in which the
listener plays a much more active role in determining both the nature
and the outcome of the communicative encounter.

If listening is behavior, then it can be taught, learned, changed, corrected, and re-learned, like any other behavior.

But even granting that listening behavior can be modified, the argument has been raised that listening is an incredibly complex process
and that we simply do not know enough about it to teach listening as
a subject. We do not deny that listening is a complicated subject, but
we do not believe that this complexity precludes us from teaching it.
The complexities of other parts of the communication process have
not prevented us from examining and teaching them. Nor should
complexity prevent us from researching and teaching the behavior we
call listening.

During the past few years the literature of speech communication
has been enriched with several books on listening. These were path-
finding volumes, introducing listening as a serious topic for study.
They were essentially exhortative in nature, failing to give any serious
consideration of the psychological processes involved in listening,
processes which must be understood if listening is to be understood.

Professor Weaver's book, **Human Listening: Processes and Behavior**
represents a real advance over earlier treatments of the subject. He
recognizes that listening is indeed an exceedingly complex behavior,
but that research in communication, psychology, sociology, and physi-
ology have given us important insights into the complexities. His is,
therefore, not a book of guesses and assumptions. His research has
produced a theory of listening behavior based on studies heretofore
unexplored by most scholars in our discipline. And from that theory
has evolved both an understanding of the role of listening in a theory
of communication, and prescriptions for teaching and learning listening.

Human Listening is divided into three conceptual areas: (1) a general presentation of listening behavior and its place in the communication process; (2) the major social and psychological processes involved in the selection and cognition of aurally received data; (3) re-
medial measures for both the speaker and the auditor.

Chapter 1 defines listening and emphasizes its necessary role in any theory of communication. Common misconceptions about listening are evaluated and reasons are presented for improving listening behavior.

Chapters 2 and 3 present cognitive processes involved in listening. The three processes of cognition are presented in Chapter 2: **selective attention,** the process by which the organism focuses its energy and awareness on one stimulus in order to ascribe meaning to it; **categorization,** the process which makes it possible to ascribe meaning to a stimulus pattern; and **fluctuation of attention,** the phenomenon which makes it difficult, often impossible, for the organism to sustain attention on any stimulus for more than a few seconds.

Chapter 3 describes and explains two organismic states which affect the three processes of cognition described in the previous chapter. These two states are the pressures of bias and the ways they affect the reception of data, and the effects of sex difference on the kinds of input data selected.

Chapters 4 and 5 are addressed to the ways in which listeners can improve their ability to receive data, and the ways in which speakers can aid their listeners. Both chapters present exercises to develop these abilities.

Professor Weaver has included two appendixes: "The Teaching and Testing of Listening" and "The Use of Compressed Speech in Research and Teaching." These essays are related to Chapters 1 and 2, and are intended for those who wish to pursue further the study of listening. Extensive bibliographies are provided at the end of each chapter.

This is not an easy book; scholarship has not been sacrificed for simplicity. Nevertheless, even the relatively unsophisticated student of speech communication will find the work valuable. And for the more advanced student the book provides an abundance of theses and conceptions which can be fruitfully discussed and tested. We believe **Human Listening: Processes and Behavior** is an extremely important contribution to our discipline.

Russel R. Windes

Ewart A. Autry

WE QUIT TALKING—AND NOW THE CUPBOARD IS BARE*

"We're talking too much," my wife announced one morning at breakfast. "But these are the first words we've said since we sat down," I protested. "I mean when we're out in public or have company," she explained. "We carry too much of the conversation. It must bore others."

I thought it over. "Well," I finally agreed, "it's true we rarely run out of words."

"And we're always eager to get them in," she continued. "We talk so much that people learn everything about us while we're learning nothing about them. So let's do something about it."

"Tape our lips?" I suggested.

She ignored that, with reason. "Let's agree to limit our part of the conversation when others are around," she said. "We'll set up some signals. When you think I'm talking too much just touch your forehead and I'll slow down. When I think you're talking too much, I'll use the same signal."

I was skeptical but willing to try. So we did. On our very next visitor.

It wasn't a successful experiment. He was a phlegmatic neighbor who never used any more words than were absolutely necessary. That, coupled with our resolve to let guests carry most of the conversation, produced long, awkward silences. Intermittently the three of us stared into our open fire and there was little sound except the crackling of my hickory logs. When our visitor had gone, my wife looked chagrined. "I kept hoping you'd talk," she said, "but I didn't know how to get you started. The only signal we agreed on was the one to cut down on the talking."

There was another repercussion from that fiasco. Our visitor reported to the neighbors that we weren't well and they kept calling to inquire about our health. "That's some reputation to have," I grumbled. "When we don't rattle on all the time, people think we're sick."

Most visitors, though, unknowingly cooperated with our new scheme. They kept the conversation rolling with no more than an occasional word from us. It was amazing how much some people talked. I commented on it one day after a visit from Dan and Ina Blake. "Dan was really wound up," I said. "I thought he'd never finish that story about the big bass he caught Christmas day."

"This is the first chance he's had to finish it," advised my wife. "Always before you've interrupted to tell some wild fish story of your own."

"And I noticed Ina got in the full account of her latest operation," I re-

* Originally published in **MINUTES**, Fall 1970, pp. 13–14. Reprinted by permission of the author and **MINUTES**, Magazine of Nationwide Insurance.

torted. "Other times you've put your stitches in before she could even begin on hers."

"It takes will power to keep your mouth shut," said my wife thoughtfully. "Especially when you have something more interesting to tell than what's being told."

The signals actually worked well and we didn't have to use them too often. But sometimes we'd let our tongues get ahead of our brains. Like when I was telling Don Duke about a bass I'd hooked. The fish was weighing about nine pounds and I had him on the way to the boat when I saw my wife touch her forehead. I immediately cut the bass down to three pounds and let him get away.

Then there's the time my wife was telling some friends about a recent vacation trip to the ocean. She was waxing poetic as she described a sunset over the water. I noticed our visitors beginning to wiggle restlessly, so I caught her eye and touched my forehead. You never saw a sun drop so quickly into the sea.

There were times when others noticed our signals. Once we were visiting friends and I was talking too much. My wife touched her forehead. When I didn't react immediately she kept touching it. In a few minutes our hostess left the room and returned with a glass of water and an aspirin. "You poor thing," she said to my wife. "You have a headache. Take this."

A few days later I had a bad crick in my neck. I went to a doctor who is a family friend. At his invitation my wife came into the consultation room. She began to tell him my various symptoms. I thought she was telling too much so I touched my forehead. The doctor noticed it immediately. "Ah, ha," he said. "Just as I thought. You have sinus trouble."

He tilted my chin and sprayed my nose with the hottest stuff I ever felt. My eyes watered for an hour. But I must have touched the right spot. My neck was better before we got home.

Our talk curb has been in effect for a year now. We've talked less and heard more. Not all of it has been worthwhile but at least it's been as good as some of the stuff we were putting out.

And we've learned one thing for certain—talk less and you'll have more company. More people came to our house this past year than in any of the thirty we've been married. One of our regular visitors said why. "I like to visit here," he beamed. "You're interesting people to talk to."

"To." Not "with."

We have a problem though. Much of our company has been at mealtime. Sometimes our pantry has been stripped to the danger point. Right now we're trying to decide whether to buy more groceries each week or forget our conversation moratorium.

When I mention the second possibility, my wife gets an eager gleam in her eyes. And come to think of it, there are a few things I'd like to say too. So, if you're planning to come to our house, you'd better hurry. Before we start talking again.

Preface

Writing a book on listening behavior has been a great pleasure for me. During the years I have taught courses in listening to graduate students, I have often concluded that although the principles and materials are difficult to comprehend, the importance of understanding listening as a vital and neglected phase of the communication process makes it imperative to expose undergraduate students to a knowledge of listening behavior. Because of the temptations to oversimplify and/or overstate, translating the theories and principles of listening behavior into clear and understandable prose has not been easy. Nevertheless, I believe this volume introduces the reader to those basic theories and principles without involving him in the many complexities that only the scholars and future scholars in the field would wish to deal with.

In planning a book, the author must always make certain assumptions about his material. One of my assumptions was that one cannot expect to change basic habits and abilities very much in a single course—or through reading a single book. Listening ability must be developed over a period of time because it requires redirecting habits and retraining skills. It is my firm belief that a student can accomplish these goals best if he has a thorough understanding of the processes of listening behavior. Consequently, much of this volume has been written to teach the student **about** listening. The remainder of the book is devoted to training the student **how to** listen more effectively and how to help others to do the same.

A second assumption I ask the reader to share with me is that listening is a type of behavior difficult both to understand and to change. Simply to describe the processes involved in listening, I must introduce the reader to concepts and a vocabulary that may not be at all a part of his experiences. I have had to use technical terms and difficult concepts from time to time. But in every case I have attempted to explain and relate the material to more understandable examples and illustrations. The obstacles may be readily overcome. A student is in college to expose his mind to new words and concepts and, through the exposure, to emerge a different person.

I urge the reader to involve himself in the exercises suggested throughout the book, particularly those in Chapters 4 and 5. My own experience suggests that these and similar exercises can produce astonishing results. Perhaps listening cannot be **taught,** but many of us are convinced that it can be **learned.**

It is my belief that the principles in this book will be supported by what is learned in many other courses in college. Studies in biology, sociology, psychology, and so forth, will not only substantiate theories about listening behavior contained in this volume; they should add materially to the reader's basic knowledge of listening.

I have included in two appendixes to this volume material on the teaching and testing of listening and the use of compressed speech in research and teaching. This material is an expanded and more technical presentation of parts of Chapters 1 and 2, and is included here for those readers who wish to pursue these subjects further.

Carl H. Weaver

Acknowledgments

It is not easy to decide who should be thanked for helping in the writing of a book. In this case, as in most, the possibility of error lies in omitting the names of people who contributed to the completion of the work. Thanks must certainly go to my wife for typing the manuscript and for spending many lonely Saturdays and Sundays while I wrote it. Dr. Paul H. Boase deserves my gratitude for giving me time to work on the manuscript. Dr. Richard Halley, Dr. Edd Sewell, and Dr. Robert Young helped me with chores around the office and Dr. Wesley Shellen and Ann Anderson with the editing of the manuscript. Finally, Dr. Russel Windes improved the book immeasurably by his questions and criticisms.

Contents

Appendixes

Human listening

PROCESSES AND BEHAVIOR

ONE

Listening behavior: an overview.

Day after day and week after week for more than two years the North Vietnamese and the Americans met in Paris, sometimes regularly and sometimes not, and heard each other talk. They were trying to end the Vietnam War. They met to bargain. They talked. They explained and redefined their positions and their demands. Sometimes their exchanges were courteous and sometimes they were insulting and vitriolic. Yet in all this time no action came of it. Did they listen to each other?

Of course they did. They listened very carefully, and they were very careful listeners. Every word and every vocal inflection was heard and carefully noted. The slightest change in a sentence or shift of voice was remembered and later analyzed. Perhaps one side was giving way a little. Did this new phrase mean more concessions would be made? If so, would the enemy move back two steps more if we pretended not to have noticed it? Or would our best strategy be an attack on this point? Careful analyses and reports were sent back to each government to be used as bases for new instructions. And the talking went on.

It would be a mistake indeed to think the negotiators were not listening or communicating. They were doing both quite well, and to think

3

they were not is to confuse both listening and communicating with agreeing. Let us spend a little time thinking about communicating and the role listening plays in the process.

The role of listening in communicating

Communicating is a process, and listening is at the very heart of it. We may define communicating as **a process that occurs when an agent receives data.** This means any kind of agent and any kind of data. We are not now talking about human beings alone, but about animals and machines too. Animals, of course, can receive information about the external world via their senses. They can receive data from their own bodies too, from internal sensors. Communication takes place, according to the definition above, whenever an animal (as the agent) thus receives data from his external or internal world. You should note that listening (the receiving of data) is the single necessary ingredient. In some situations an agent may receive data when, from a common-sense point of view, there is no sender. You may get a great deal of information, for example, by looking at inanimate objects on someone's desk. You may say, perhaps, that the objects are sending messages, or you may say (as some people do) that the owner is sending the messages—because they would not be on the desk if he hadn't placed them there—but both claims seem a little foolish.

Some machines can also send or receive data, both from men and from other machines. The big computer at Beltsville, Maryland, and its twin sister in Houston, Texas, receive data constantly when NASA is sending a rocket to the moon. The thermostat on the wall of your room periodically sends messages to the furnace or some other part of the heating system, telling it to do something. When it does, and warms up the room, the thermostat collects data (temperature) from the air of the room. Biologists consider RNA to be a communication agent, carrying messages to molecules that receive the information and respond.

Does it surprise you to hear that such nonhuman agents can receive data? If it does, it is probably because you have always thought of information as verbal or numerical. It is not, of course. By the time even verbal information reaches your central nervous system, as you will see later, it is in a form not significantly different from the data sent from Beltsville to Houston or from data sent by a sending agent on a rocket speeding to the moon or back to earth.

But since we are talking about **human** communication in this book, we should add the word "human" to our definition immediately before the word "agent." Then our definition allows communication to take place **when a human agent receives data.** Human beings, of course, can receive information from nonhuman sources. The condition of your room or a long blond hair on your shoulder is data to a human observer. It communicates something. It follows that the sender of the message need not be human, and the sending itself need not be intentional. Indeed, we are constantly sending messages to others that we would not send if we only knew about them. Sometimes we strive to send only a certain kind of message to someone in order to impress him, but at the same time other messages that we do not know we are sending give him a more realistic picture of us than we want him to have. Consider your first date, for example, with a person you really want to impress. You "put your best foot forward." You try your best to conceal all the negative things you know about yourself in order to deceive the other. As you get acquainted better and better, this self-guard falls and you begin honestly to reveal yourself.

But, again, this is a book about listening, so we had better narrow our concept of listening to human reception of aurally input data. It seems obvious that no human communication takes place unless someone receives the message. A talker in a room alone is communicating with no one—except, perhaps, himself. A listener can receive data from many sources, but a talker talks to empty air unless someone receives it.

So let us define what we mean by **listening.**

A definition of listening

We will say that listening has occurred **when a human organism receives data aurally.** Of course, we could broaden this definition by deleting the word "human." Other organisms listen too; but this book is about human listening. We could narrow the definition by adding the word "verbal" just before the word "data." This would restrict the definition to the reception of one kind of aurally input data; there are other kinds that are part of the listening process too. We have already restricted the definition to data input aurally. We will not consider visual data at all. This should not surprise you, since this is a book on listening. Although all the senses work together, often simultaneously, to input data into the system during the process of communication, we will study only one of them. This is not unreasonable. A book on the reception of communicative data that concerned all modes of input (touch, taste, smell, vision, hearing, plus the interoceptor senses) would not be a book on listening at all, but a book on communication.

You should note the word "data" in the definition, which you may translate to "information" if you like. Aurally input data may be considered to be of three kinds: (1) verbal data, (2) vocal data, and (3) other kinds of sounds. Of course, you should realize that nothing is "input" into the system aurally except sound waves, which strike the tympanic membrane (eardrum) in the ear and cause it to vibrate very nearly exactly as the sound waves do. The energy in these waves is transduced into electrical energy and carried via the eighth nerve to the central nervous system, where a very complicated process occurs. This process is called **cognitive structuring** and will be described in some detail in Chapters 2 and 3. The data received by the organism are thus the characteristics of a complex wave pattern. That is all. You have probably studied complex sound waves in your science classes.

It is not necessary to say much here about the data sent by a verbal message. Such data will be the central concern of this book. When a person talking to you utters the sound pattern for the word "come," the sound waves strike your tympanic membrane and set the entire process in motion. Since you know your own referent for that sound pattern, you "know what it means." You have received some data. What you do about the data is another matter. Let us assume that the single word "come" is a command. Whether you obey it or not does not concern the process of listening. You have "heard" it, which means you have received and attended to the data. The listening process concerns only the selecting of such stimulus data in order to "receive" it and the cognitive structuring of it. If several people are talking to you at the same time, it is necessary for you to select the words of one talker and listen to them. The others will not be heard although, as you will read later, an unattended verbal message may not be entirely neglected.

You should note that the term **receiving** includes both selecting and structuring, or handling, the data. This means, as you will learn further in Chapters 2 and 3, that the data will be stored somewhere in your brain and thus will be remembered. Data that are not selected for attention do not usually enter the memory system and thus are not really received.

Vocal data may sometimes be as important as verbal data to the listener. The voice quality, inflections, etc., often tell the listener how to interpret the verbal message, what the intent and condition of the talker are, whether the message is a command, a request, or a question. Simply by hearing the vocal cues, a listener can infer many meanings from a verbal message spoken in a language he does not know. Animals understand messages from humans by listening to vocal cues. We can even estimate quite accurately the mental adjustment of a talker when all the consonants in his speech have been filtered out and we cannot understand his words. Although, as noted above, the primary interest of this book will be the verbal message, you should not forget that the way words are said contributes to the meaning you get when you listen to them. It is part of the data you hear.

Finally, listening is concerned also with many other kinds of sounds, although they will not be a major concern of this book. A fire siren, a barking dog, a belch—all communicate meaning to you if you are listening. They are part of the aurally input data that help you adjust and react to your environment. And they may be part of the human communication process, perhaps when they become distractions that you must override as when a friend who is drawing a diagram for you breaks his pencil or gasps to show his exasperation.

Aspects of the listening process. How well a person **can** listen and how well he **does** listen are not the same thing. Furthermore, how well he does listen depends on two factors: his listening habits and his willingness to listen. These three aspects of listening—capacity, willingness, and habits—will be merged most of the time throughout this book, and you will do well to understand them now and keep them in mind as you read.

1. The capacity to listen concerns the ability to select and structure input data and thus remember it. Listening-improvement exercises are usually concerned with this aspect of listening. Ability depends partly on intelligence, of course, which tends to place some maximum limit on the rate and quality of data handling. General sophistication and knowledge of the subject of the message are also factors in this aspect of listening. You cannot handle very fast data on some difficult subject about which you know nothing. This is one reason why children's ability to listen improves as they grow older. Previous experience in handling difficult information also affects present ability. If you have never listened to anything except remarks about the

weather, it is likely that you will find information about difficult subjects hard to handle. But if you have had a great deal of experi-ence in listening to thoughtful speeches and conversations, it will be easier for you to handle most data sent to you.

2. Willingness to listen is probably as important as capacity to listen. High ability that is never used is of no benefit to anyone. Unwillingness to listen may be both general and selective. Some peo-ple almost never listen; they talk too much, they daydream, or they seem never to pay attention to anyone else. Others may be very good listeners on some subjects or at some times but be quite unwilling to listen to other subjects or at other times. When we have heard a great deal about some subject, we often become bored with it and do not want to hear of it again. This may sometimes be a useful form of conservation of energy, but it tends to block the input of new data. Perhaps the most frustrating and harmful cause of unwillingness to listen is the one demonstrated by people who want their own way and are simply unwilling to listen to any other proposal. The many pressure groups in our country today tend to act this way. A group of workers pressing their employer for higher wages or more fringe benefits are usually like this. They are convinced before management begins to speak that money is plentiful, and therefore management often talks to people who are not listening. Students who demand control over a university budget of a hundred million dollars are often unwilling to listen to arguments against such a delegation of authority. A husband and wife on their way to estrangement are often unwilling to listen to each other. Their problem is usually not an inability to listen to each other but an unwillingness. A marriage counselor who can overcome this unwillingness can often resolve the confict.

3. Finally, everyone has developed habits of listening that exert strong control over his behavior. A child reared in a nagging home will soon learn to close his ears to repeated unwelcome messages. His behavior is usually extended to such messages outside the home and generalized to all kinds of messages. A child who does not need to listen because he knows nothing bad will happen to him will develop poor habits. Even a wife whose husband always "takes care of her" will develop poor habits, and not merely in listening. However they start and for whatever reason, poor listening habits cause many of us to use our listening capacity much less well than we could.

There are, thus, these three aspects of listening: the capacity to handle aurally input data, the willingness to listen, and listening habits. You should keep these aspects constantly in mind as you read this book.

Kinds of data. There are two kinds of data in a verbal message: explicit and implicit.

1. Explicit data are said. It is easy to understand this concept if you think of verbal data. Explicit data are what is actually verbalized. If the message is written, the data may be seen on the page, pointed to, verified. If it is spoken, it is the data which actually reach your ears.

2. Implicit data are not said but implied. Such data are generated by a listener from what he actually hears. When he does this, he is making an inference, and his inferences are sometimes more important than the data he hears.

For example, if one woman says to another, "I like your hat. I liked it last year too," you may be sure the intended meaning is not what is said. When you are, while listening, trying to decide why the talker is telling you what he is telling, you are searching for a good inference. A high school English teacher once backed another teacher into a corner of the office and spent twenty minutes explaining why she had given the superintendent's daughter an A. The **reason** for her behavior was more important than what she said. And the reason had to be inferred. It was never said explicitly.

Much of what we mean—and often what we want the listener to hear—remains unsaid, or implicit. We want him to understand something we do not want or dare to say. We may even make such implications by saying nothing. If someone says to you, "Mr. Jones is a splendid fellow, isn't he?" and you remain silent, you have said something implicitly. Your listener, waiting in vain for an explicit message, decides that there is only one reason you have not given him one, and he makes an inference. The inference he makes is probably what the "silent talker" intended.

Thus a good listener hears the explicit data, but he "hears" the implicit data too. If he is really a good listener, he knows which is explicit and which is implicit, and he makes the inferences he should.

Is listening a unitary skill or a collection of subskills? Thus far, we have been defining and describing listening as if we were quite sure what the process is like. This is not really so. Ever since communication scholars have been studying listening and trying to teach people to do it better, they have been unable to agree on what to teach. Of necessity, when such a scholar sits at his desk and plans a course in listening improvement, he must decide just what kinds of activities should go on in the class and what objectives he should pursue. Thus one early study set the objective of teaching students to listen better to college lectures. The researcher collected a great many such lectures on tapes, played the tapes to his students, and tested them on each lecture to see if they had improved. Another believed the skill of taking good notes on a speech would improve listening. Another had his students engage in conversations and at intervals asked a listener to repeat to the talker what he had just said.

We may call these activities **subskills,** part of the general skill of listening. Certainly, we listen in many different situations, to many kinds of messages, with many different purposes, and to many different kinds of talkers. There are so many possibilities involved that it is difficult to say just what kind of human behavior we should call listening behavior. Here is a list—long but not complete—of behaviors communication scholars have tried to improve. You should study it carefully.

To get main ideas
To hear the facts
To make valid inferences
To get the central theme
To retain pertinent content
To identify the main and supporting ideas
To perceive differences between similarly worded statements
To identify correct English usage
To use contextual clues to determine "word meanings"
To comprehend oral instructions
To hear details
To hear difficult material
To adjust to the speaker
To listen under bad conditions
To resist the influence of emotion-laden words and arguments
To take notes
To structuralize a speech
To prevent the facts from interfering with hearing the main idea
To improve concentration by use of special techniques
To hear speaker's words
To develop curiosity
To follow directions

To judge relevancy
To recognize topic sentences and to associate each topic
    sentence with some previous bit of knowledge
To recognize what the speaker wants the listener to do
To understand how words can create a mood
To understand connotative meanings
To predict what will happen next
To understand denotative meanings
To identify speaker attitudes
To get meaning from imagery
To notice sequences of ideas and details
To check for the accuracy of new information
To avoid the effects of projection
To evaluate and apply material presented
To introspect and analyze one's own listening disabilities
To judge validity and adequacy of main ideas
To discriminate between fact and fancy
To judge whether the speaker has accomplished his purpose
To recognize self-contradictions by the speaker
To be aware of persuasive devices used by the speaker

It is not easy to say that any of the subskills of listening in the list above is unrelated to listening, although some of them seem marginal. If we decide that listening is such a set of subskills, then perhaps we should teach all of them. Many people have taught a few of them and called their courses listening courses. All the published listening tests measure some of these subskills, and since they measure different subskills, they do not agree with each other. That is, you may score well on the Brown-Carlsen Listening Comprehension test but less well on the test called Sequential Steps in Educational Progress.

It has been suggested that all these subskills depend on a single, more basic operation—reliable, valid, and rapid cognitive structuring of aurally input data. We are talking here about the **capacity** to listen, not listening habits or the willingness to listen. All the subskills listed above may be dependent on the one basic ability to handle the information sent in messages. Perhaps a technique of teaching that would improve that skill would also improve all the subskills in the list.

It is not difficult to believe this. Many reading-improvement courses operate largely on this hypothesis, and some of them have been successful. It might be presumed that improving your skill in handling data from the printed page would improve your skill in handling aurally input data. However, this has not been demonstrated. It may be that we will never be able to demonstrate it, but we do have some evidence that data input aurally is not handled in the same way as data input visually.

The position taken in this book is that listening capacity is a unitary process of handling data. Perhaps after you have studied Chapters 2 and 3 you will agree.

Listening and reading are not the same process. Finally, in defining and explaining listening, you should understand what was alluded to above—that listening and reading are separate processes.

Scholars have found that when large batteries of tests are administered to groups of people and a factor analysis made, the listening and reading tests produce two different factors, not heavily loaded on each other. That is, they do not overlap, as might be expected. Both factors depend on intelligence and probably on some other variables. But when several tests of reading and of listening are administered, the reading tests correlate highly with each other but not with the listening tests; and the listening tests correlate highly with each other but not with the reading tests; this simply means that the tests tap different skills.

Finally, one study demonstrated that when we read a story and when we hear it, we mark different items correctly on a test. No one knows quite why this is so, but it implies different processes for the two kinds of behavior—reading and listening.

In this section devoted to a definition of listening, you should have developed an understanding of listening as **a process that takes place when a human organism receives data aurally.** You should understand that listening involves verbal, vocal, and other sounds; that skill as a listener includes the capacity to handle data, the willingness to hear it, and previously formed listening habits; and that the data in a message may be either explicit or implicit. Finally, you should have some understanding of the question of listening subskills versus the unitary process of listening, and you should know that listening and reading are different processes.

Time spent in listening

Most people are unaware of the proportion of their time they spend in listening. After all, listening is neither so dramatic nor so noisy as talking. The talker is the center of attention for all listeners. His behavior is overt and vocal, and he hears and notices his own behavior, whereas listening activity often seems like merely being there—doing nothing. Thus we are likely to remember how much of the time we talk but forget how much we listen.

Several studies have been done at various levels to determine the proportion of a human being's time that is spent in the four aspects of the communication process. Rankin (1926, 1930)* found that of the time 68 adults spent in communication, they spent 45 percent in listening, 30 percent in talking, 16 percent in reading, and 9 percent in writing. Bird had female college students keep records and found that they spent 42 percent of their time listening, 25 percent talking, 15 percent reading, and 18 percent writing. Wilt studied 530 elementary school pupils from grades 1 through 6 and found that they spent 57.5 percent of their time listening.

Obviously, the proportion of time students spend in listening depends on the kind of material being presented and the method of presentation. Also, the amount of time spent in listening by lower-grade, elementary school pupils would be greater than at higher levels because of their inability or low ability to read and write. The similarity between college students and out-of-school adults, however, is striking, and it has been concluded by most scholars concerned with this problem that people in general spend about 45 percent of their communicative time in listening as opposed to about 25 percent in talking. Few studies like these have been reported since the 1950s. It is possible, but not likely, that a new study would give us different figures. It certainly seems sometimes as if everyone today is talking at once—college students, senators, proponents of various causes, etc.

These figures, however, are impressive. For several centuries we have devoted our study and teaching to the expressive part of the oral communicative process, which we use only about half as much of the time as we use the receptive skills. Now we are studying the whole process.

The need for good listening

Listening capacity, or ability, improves with increasing sophistication and age, two factors that may have about the same effect on the

* Sources for all research mentioned in the text may be found in the bibliography at the end of each chapter. Publication dates are noted only when more than one work by the same author appears in the bibliography.

listening process. We would expect someone who has a wide stock of information and has had considerable practice in listening to be able to understand many different kinds of messages better than a child who may not know what the speaker is talking about. Wright found this effect between grades 2 and 4. Hampleman found it between grades 4 and 6, as did M. Johnson. Brown and Carlsen and Caffrey (**Education,** 1955) found it between grades 9 and 12. Erickson found it among college freshmen, and Carver found it between adults with a good educational background and adults with a poor educational background.

Rossiter studied upper-level undergraduates and graduate students between the ages of twenty and sixty and found that at the upper age levels listening capacity fell off significantly. In fact, the fall-off was linear across the entire age range. Like the other studies cited above, Rossiter's study was done under testing conditions. His results indicate, therefore, that although the **capacity** for listening rises linearly with age and experience, at some point it begins to decline.

It should be noted that we have been talking about the capacity—or ability—to listen. Nichols and Stevens demonstrated that, although students' listening ability may increase as they grow older and learn more, their **habits** of listening may deteriorate. They reported a study in which schoolteachers stopped in the middle of their lectures and asked, "What was I talking about?" In the first grades, 90 percent of the pupils could answer this question, but the proportion decreased as the grade levels rose. Eighty percent of the second graders could answer it, 43.7 percent of the junior high school students, and 28 percent of the high school students. Obviously, as this kind of population grows older, they use less and less of their capacity for listening, at least in the classroom. It is possible that they listen quite well in other situations, but unfortunately the need for good listening often—if not most of the time—occurs in situations where the message is somewhat less than fascinating. However, a person should be able to listen well to anything he needs to, not merely to what he likes.

Nichols and Stevens believe people in our culture are taught **not** to listen. Mother reminds Johnny to wear his boots and not to forget his lunch, but she watches him so closely that he learns quickly enough that he need not listen at all. Mother will not let him forget. The time finally comes when his exasperated mother declares, "You would forget your head if it weren't fastened on." When Johnny gets to school he is still further conditioned against listening. The principal makes announcements each morning over a public-address system, the teacher repeats them, and they are often posted on a bulletin board. Yet the number of students who go to the wrong place, for example, to buy football tickets—after all these oral and written announcements— is sometimes appalling. They don't listen. They don't need to. Someone will tell them again and they will get to the right place in the end.

How many television commercials say something only once? Usually the information is simplified, repeated in several ways, and even printed on the screen so that no one needs to listen much at all. And if we miss it the first time, we can always wait a few minutes. The entire sequence will be repeated again.

In 1872 Mutual of New York installed a big clock on the top of its new building. A great deal of publicity preceded the starting of the clock, and many New Yorkers were watching in the street. To the consternation of the clock expert, the clock would not move because of a cracked gear. Aware of the importance of the event, he hung his watch on a peg and instructed a workman to move the hands of the clock every minute, as if it were running. Then he removed the gear in order to send it to Boston and get a replacement. So the clock "started." The clock expert, after all these arrangements, went to the company's New York agent to tell him what was happening. He had barely started when the agent leaped out of his chair and lurched around the room, swearing. "We'll be the laughingstock of the town," he shouted. "Our competitors will have a field day. Finally he stopped at the window and looked at the clock. "But the clock is going!" he cried in amazement.

"Of course," said the clock expert. "You didn't let me finish my story."

Cardozo has suggested that our entire culture conditions us not to listen but to talk. The silent act of listening is no match for the "bellowing and visible salvos which daily are fired" at us. Indeed, the way to impose one's will on others, which seems increasingly to have become the objective of many pressure groups, is to talk, yell, shout, and not to give the other a chance to reply. Of course, everyone would like to have everything go the way he wants. We have generally assumed that the way to do this is through persuasion, which to most people means talking—verbal manipulation. One cannot persuade, it seems, by listening, and the people who act as if they believe this travel in good company. Speech scholars themselves often teach persuasion as an expressive act. There is probably no single course in persuasion in which students are taught to persuade by listening. Yet there are ways; often it is possible to secure agreement with your position by simple and gentle questioning of someone with an opposing viewpoint and listening to him explain his position. If he is wrong, he is likely to see his own fallacies, especially if your listening behavior is courteous enough to be nonthreatening. Simple listening will also do this at times, without any questioning at all.

So we hear too little and understand less than we could. Someone has said that if we would only listen more, we would not only have more friends but we would also learn something, and we would understand others better. An article in **Fortune** ("Is Anybody Listening?") suggested that by **not** listening we create great gaps between ourselves and others with whom we wish to have understanding. In an article entitled "Why Good Men Quit," **Changing Times** contended that the capable men in a business, the ones the employer would be loath to lose, want the employer to listen to them. If they cannot get him to hold still long enough for them to present an idea they think good or if, after they have presented the idea, he asks a question that indicates he has not listened at all but only pretended to, the good men will leave. They will go to another job where, they hope, someone **will** listen to them. Planty and Machaver have written, ". . . by far the most effective method of tapping the ideas of subordinates is sympathetic listening in the many day-to-day informal contacts within the department and outside the workplace."

There is no better illustration of the need for better listening than the conficts that have been going on in America in recent years between the majority and minority groups, between youth and adults, between university students and almost all the rest of the population, between women and the world, etc.

It is easy for a middle-aged American to decide that student dissidents are led by communists and thenceforth reject anything they say. It is easy for him to believe that the young men who oppose the Vietnam War are simply too lazy or too scared to fight for their country, or that their organized opposition to an industry contributing to the military-government-industrial complex is simply another communist front, probably inspired by Hanoi and communist China. It is much more difficult to listen to the statements made by such young people and to understand why they are made.

At the same time, it is also easy for a youth to believe that anyone over thirty has been brought up in a culture that cannot understand him. He easily rejects statements that this is probably the best country in the world in which to live or that completely destroying our military forces might result in a situation like the one China faced at the time of the Boxer Rebellion. (She was invaded by two great military powers, the United States and Great Britain, to preserve their trade there, and China was helpless because she had reduced her own armed forces to impotence and could not fight back.) It is easy for youth to reject the statement that one deserves to keep what he can earn in this world and that he can earn quite a bit if he prepares well and works hard. It is much more difficult for youth to listen carefully to such statements in order to understand the assumptions on which they rest and their implications.

Thus we have seen in our time situations in which capable and wise men have been shouted down, driven from the platform, insulted, and often pelted with filth because some people **don't want to listen.** In one case, a leading figure of the Republican Party was insulted by the audience when he spoke, by invitation, to its national convention. We have also seen cases where so-called hard hats have driven youths from the streets. We have seen two sides in many conflicts with hardened positions who have no desire to listen to or understand each other.

Sometimes listening might have helped. One young Women's Liberation member made the statement that employment should be open to all people regardless of sex, that women or men should be employed as if they were asexual. Several listeners objected to this statement, suggesting that there must be some limitations on it and asking her if she would not like to soften it. She responded vigorously that there were no limitations and that she had meant it exactly as she had said it. One questioner posed this problem for her: "Suppose you had a twelve-year-old daughter and you and your husband were going away on a trip for a week, leaving the daughter at home. But you do not want to leave her alone, so you decide to hire someone to stay with her. Would you really hire someone without regard to sex? Would you be willing to hire a nineteen-year-old boy to stay with her for a week?" The reply was astonishing: "Of course I would. I would hire without regard to sex. If anything happened, I would consider it my daughter's fault and not the result of the sex of the baby-sitter." This answer illustrates the unwillingness of one person to listen—to **really** listen

—to others. And her failure to listen and thus to perceive an important fallacy in her position insulated her from what we might call the truth. She was wrong, but she may never know it unless she begins to listen.

It might be said, of course, that the young lady did listen but did not agree, as the North Vietnamese and Americans did in the Paris peace talks. Such a conclusion would seem doubtful to everyone in the room at the time. It seemed more likely that she simply had not "handled" the input data so as to perceive the rather deplorable implications involved. She had heard the words and responded to the words—as we do when we read a paragraph in a book without getting any meaning from it because our minds are wandering—but she had not perceived the meaning. Only a profligate person would accept such a fate for her twelve-year-old daughter, and the young lady in this situation was a fine person. It seemed obvious that she did not get any meaning from the words she heard.

The refusal of someone to listen may lead to exaggeration and violence. The cause of improvement in our ecological environment—often simply called ecology—is an example. For many years this cause was preached by only a few people. Then the chorus grew, but little if anything was done because the people who could have done something about it did not listen. The claims grew larger and more expansive as the number of adherents grew. One of them was that life on this planet would be extinguished by 1975. The number of dimensions of the problem grew, too, until the problem embraced not merely air and water pollution but sounds and sights—even art forms judged unpalatable by someone. Finally, some violence resulted, as in the case where one man dumped a bucketful of sewer effluent on an office floor of the company that created it. Essentially, such problems are caused by the fact that people who should have listened did not.

There is also the story about the young man and woman who wanted to marry but whose parents discouraged it. They committed suicide and the young man left a note for his father: ". . . I had so much to say to you, so many things I wanted to talk about."

All these are major and dramatic and violent results of not listening. Wanting to listen should take place in common and prosaic circumstances too. Listening should take precedence over talking whenever the person we are with wants to talk. We should not merely listen to what he says but draw him out. Rarely does a talker express all his reasons and meanings and feelings in one small part of an interchange.

After his initial comment a listener should question, explore, rephrase. He should become a listener, not of a sentence but of a half hour's explanation. He would know then what the other thinks and how he feels, and he will be the wiser for it.

The reasons for good listening presented thus far have been rather general and idealistic. They are of great concern to you as a college student and young adult, and they should become more important to you as you grow older. But there are some less idealistic and more practical reasons why you should want to improve your listening while you are in college.

1. The first and most obvious of these is that by listening you will learn more. If you could remember everything your instructors say and retrieve it at any time, you would be in one sense a perfect listener. Obviously, you cannot do this. When examination time comes around you cannot reproduce very much of what your instructor has told you, and your marks suffer to some degree from this inability. To be sure, you learn a great deal in college by reading, but you would be foolish to skip all classes in which the instructor lectures and to expect to learn the subject by reading. You should hear everything the instructor says and try to remember all of it. And the better you do this, the better student you will be.

2. Another reason for learning to listen better is that you will become a better informed and more sophisticated person. It does not make you more sophisticated to tell others what you know. Your talking only helps them. But if you develop such a curiosity about all things that when you meet someone who knows something you do not, you can listen to and learn from him, you will quickly develop a great stock of information and understanding about a great many things. You will, in short, become a sophisticated person without expending much effort at all. It will be a pleasure thus to learn, and your listening habits will improve as your knowledge and curiosity grow. The good listener is sometimes surprised at the good ideas he gets when he listens.

3. Another good reason for becoming a better listener is that you will be liked and respected by all who talk to you. You will find yourself sought after and welcomed as a friend and companion. Furthermore, since more people will like you, you will like more people. We like people who like us. By listening, we compliment the person to whom we listen. Our behavior tells him we think him a worthy person.

4. Again, everyone needs careful listeners. Sometimes we need to verbalize aloud, and doing this without a listener seems a little silly. This talking to a listener often takes the form of catharsis, but it is also a way of maintaining contact with reality. We sometimes do not know the value of an idea until we say it aloud to someone else and see how he values it. Sometimes merely exposing an idea to the light of day enables the talker to evaluate it better himself. A good listener will help another person to perform all these functions for himself, and the talker will be grateful indeed. He has found a friend who thinks him worth listening to.

Of course, you should understand that listening is not the only ingredient for friendship and likableness. There are others. But careful, considerate, patient, and curious listening is one of the most important.

5. Good listening will make you a more dependable person. You will follow directions better, make fewer errors, reduce the number of times you say foolish things, and in general become the kind of person others will ask for advice or directions. If your husband or wife asks you to bring a pair of pliers and a screwdriver, you will not bring only a screwdriver. You will not be likely, as a nurse did in a large hospital in New York, to put the salt beside the sugar so that accidentally it was later mixed into babies' formulae. You will remember dates of examinations in your classes and what material will be tested, you will remember when term papers are due and what they should be like, and you will be at the right place at the right time— because you listened when instructions and explanations were made. The world needs more dependable people, and it rewards them.

6. Finally, good listening will spare you many embarrassments. Doubtless you have had to ask someone what his name was because you weren't listening when he told you. Or you have wanted to know where he lives or what he does and you cannot remember, although you can remember that he did tell you. Or you have been daydreaming (not listening) in class when the instructor asked you a question that you did not hear at all. Or you have done something in a way you were told not to do it. Doubtless you have had enough experiences of this kind to realize that if you were a good listener, life would sometimes be happier.

Thus good listening may make our world a better place, and it may also make you a more effective person.

The limits of listening

One limitation on our listening is that we cannot hear everything. Psychologists know that no organism can handle all the data input to the system. The human organism has five kinds of exteroceptors (called senses) and several kinds of interoceptors (for example, proprioception, which is thousands of little sensors buried in the muscles and internal organs, keeping us constantly informed of muscle movements and the condition of our bodies). When the organism is awake, that is, in a state of general arousal or vigilance, all these systems are sending data upward to the central nervous system. This will be discussed in some detail in Chapter 2. At this point it is important to understand that the central nervous system cannot handle all the data sent to it by even one of the exteroceptors, for example, hearing. Much of the data must be discarded in order for some of it to be attended, its meaning perceived, and a response perhaps made.

In some of the literature on listening writers seem to deplore the fact that we do not hear everything said to us. We cannot expect to. We can only hope to hear more.

We know that we do not hear as much as we could. Knower demonstrated that people score better on listening achievement tests after hearing a message when they know in advance that they are going to be tested than when they think they are just supposed to listen. This suggests that we usually listen well below our optimal ability. The condition is well known in reading too. Although the average reading ability of American citizens is well above the eighth-grade level, most popular and widely read magazines are written at this level.

Vernon found that 50 percent of his adults comprehended and retained very little of what they heard. College students marked only half the items correctly on tests made by J. I. Brown (1950) and Nichols (1949). Cartier found that college students marked only 25 percent of his test items correctly. Unfortunately, many writers in the field picked up Cartier's figure and have been writing that people hear only 25 percent of what a talker says to them. This is nonsense, of course. What Cartier found was that the students scored 25 percent on his tests. No one knows how hard his tests were. If his tests had been easier, his subjects might have averaged 75 percent, and if they had been harder, 15 percent. Furthermore, in order to compute a proportion one must have a number in the denominator. This number in the case at hand would be the **amount of data sent.** We have no way of computing this (Weaver and Weaver). No one can ever know, in the sense we are using the term **information** here, how much information is contained in any message. Information Theory measures something quite different. Horowitz and Berkowitz as well as Sincoff have made some small beginnings in computing the amount of meaning in messages, but the method is not yet either satisfactory or widely used, and none of the researchers cited earlier used it.

Another limit on the concept of listening is that **listening does not mean agreement.** Perhaps the one person we should listen to most carefully is the person who disagrees with us. It is always possible that our opponent is largely right, and listening may bring changes in our own position. But listening does not imply or require such changes. We may listen carefully and at length to the presentation of our opponent. We may question; we may explore; we may do our best to hold our own biases in abeyance as we try to see the world through his eyes. And we may, after all this, decide that our own position is the better and cling to it still. This does not mean we did not listen.

Unfortunately, many people, both orally and in print, seem to say that unless the listener ends the interchange in agreement with the talker, he has not listened. All the talking has failed. "I cannot talk with that man," you may hear someone say. "He just doesn't listen."

Such an attitude is naive. Although we cannot expect everyone who listens to us to adopt our way of life, this attitude is often displayed in the verbal-conflict situations discussed earlier in this chapter. Students will not listen to college administrators, or the administrators will not listen to the students. The President will not listen to the people who explain to him why he should pull all American troops out of Vietnam in a week. A white professor will not listen to a black student who explains that he should get a good mark on the examination even though he failed it. A member of Women's Liberation cannot get some other women to listen to her, and certainly Norman Mailer will not listen to her. Since he has written a book attacking the Women's Liberation movement, who could expect him to change his position?

The development of the study of listening

Training in one aspect of communication began a long time ago, probably reaching its peak during the days of the Greek city–states. Here the citizenry practiced the art of speaking to juries of their peers in courts of justice, and the success of their efforts was determined by who won the case. Such speaking was quite important in a pure democracy, and skill in courtroom speaking was developed to a high degree.

The skill developed there was what we now call the **expressive** skill. In large part, it consisted of preparing a good speech. Attention was focused on the words, the arguments, and their arrangement within the speech. Later the Romans continued the study of this part of the communicative process, then the French and English. By the time the study of rhetoric reached America, it concerned not only the composition of the speech itself but the delivery of it, including the quality of the voice and the use of gestures. The Delsarte system, for example, was exclusively confined to gestures and was a highly standardized and systematized set of instructions to a speaker about the ways he should move about on the platform.

At various times in the study and teaching of speech, attention to these rather peripheral aspects of rhetoric waxed and waned. Sometimes close attention was paid to the political and social setting of a speech; that is, someone would set out to discover why some great speaker used the arguments he did. Sometimes a study was done to describe the climate of the times, which was really an effort to describe the audience. The one thread of concern, however, that has persisted steadily from the days of the Greeks to these days is the study of the expressive aspect of the oral communication process.

It was not until the 1940s in America that scholars began to realize that the oral communication process also has a **receptive** aspect. Both the expressive and receptive processes had long been taught in English classes. Much attention had been given to both reading and writing. Listening, however, had generally been considered something everyone knows how to do and does well enough. When a little child entered school, it was assumed he already knew how to listen and his teachers expected him to do it as well as anyone else. After all, he had been doing it for six years already. If he did it less well than others, he was probably given a dunce cap or suffered some other kind of punishment; his failure to hear what went on in the classroom was attributed to lack of intelligence if not to mischief. Perhaps part of it was also attributed to an unwillingness to listen and his punishment was designed to make him "pay attention."

Increasingly, speech scholars in America began to realize that in studying only the expressive aspect of oral communication they were neglecting the very crux of the process. Communication does not take place because a public speaker says beautiful words in a remarkably attractive sequence with pear-shaped tones and graceful gestures. Indeed, he could do all this while completely alone in an auditorium. Communication takes place when a listener hears some message; that is, when an organism receives data aurally. Without the listener, there is no communication at all—except of the talker to himself— and the quality of the listening probably determines more than any other factor how much communication takes place.

Thus the concept of **speech** developed into the concept of **communication**. In 1950 several score teachers of speech who had begun to see the need for this change met in Washington, D.C., and established the National Society for the Study of Communication, now called the International Communication Association. The Society established the **Journal of Communication**, which started publication in 1951. In the early pages of this journal are the initial scholarly studies of the listening process and the teaching of listening. The early studies of Bird, Brown, Nichols, and others were published in this journal.

It should not be imagined, however, that only this journal and only these scholars have studied listening. Especially in psychology, much excellent work has been done, some of it before 1950, usually under some other name. Some of these studies are listed in the bibliographies at the ends of the chapters in this book. Interest in the efficiency of the listening process is now both wide and deep. It is not confined to universities but has become the focus of some concern in the public schools, in industry, in politics, and in homes. Everywhere, it seems, people are concerned with a situation in which few seem to listen but everyone talks. You are beginning the study of a kind of human behavior that almost everyone thinks important.

Summary

In this chapter you have read an overview of the process of listening, including a definition of the term as it will be used in this book. Later chapters will go into the process of listening, what you can do to improve your listening, and what you can do as a talker to help others to listen better.

The first three chapters have been designed to teach you something **about** listening. It is doubtful that you can learn enough in one course to change your habit patterns remarkably. It is more likely that changes will come over a period of several years or even the next decade. You will improve most if you understand what the process is really like. Knowing that, you can guide your own behavior toward better listening during the next decade or even the rest of your life. This is true of your other communication behaviors too, for example, public speaking and conference leadership and participation.

Chapter 2 will explain what goes on in your central nervous system as you listen. Chapter 3 will discuss two important variables that affect the processes you will have studied in Chapter 2: the effects of biases and of sex on the selection and handling of aurally input data. Chapters 4 and 5 will reveal what we know and what we think about ways to improve listening in any communicative situation. Should you want to read the original studies on which this book is based, you will find the bibliographies at the end of each chapter useful.

Thus this is not merely a how-to-do-it book. It has in it the information you will need to continue to improve your listening long after you leave the classroom.

Exercises

1. If you have or can borrow a stop watch, keep a record of your talking and listening time during an hour when you are in a communicative situation, for example, drinking coffee with a group of other students. You will need a notebook in which to make entries under the headings **talking** and **listening.**

   If you do this in various kinds of situations, you will probably get different results. You may vary the number of people in the group or your own activities and theirs. If everyone is eating, for example, the talking–listening patterns may change.

2. Use your stop watch to time someone else's talking–listening patterns. It is important not to let him know what you are timing.

3. Let someone else time your talking–listening patterns.

4. Listen to a discussion or argument between two people on opposing sides of an issue—the Vietnam War, the use of marijuana, Women's Liberation, or any such current topic on which both feel strongly. Count (a) the total number of interactions (number of times one person speaks) and (b) the

number of questions asked that were really designed to help the asker understand the other better. Compute the proportion of total interactions that represents the number of interactions designed to gain information.

5. Try to find a radical on some subject. Listen to him until you hear him say something that you can deny and support your denial with facts that he should know. Then try to get him to change his statement. What do you think is going on in him as he answers?

6. After you have listened to someone, try to decide whether the meaning you got from his statements was explicit or implicit. If you decide the most important part of the meaning was implicit, try to decide whether you made a good inference or a poor one.

7. When you walk away from someone after a conversation with him, reflect on your **willingness** to listen. Did you really want to hear what he had to say, or were you more anxious to talk yourself?

8. Try to catch yourself talking simply because you want to "talk something out," to hear yourself say it aloud and thus evaluate it better.

9. Catch yourself remembering, after a conversation with someone, something he said that you paid no attention to at the time. How can you remember it now if you paid no attention to it then?

Bibliography

Abrams, Arnold. "The Relation of Listening and Reading Comprehension to Skill in Message Structuralization," **Journal of Communication,** 16 (1966), 116.

Bakan, Paul. "Some Reflections on Listening Behavior," **Journal of Communication,** 6 (1956), 108.

————, and B. T. Leckart. "Complexity Judgments of Photographs and Looking Time," **Perceptual and Motor Skills,** 21 (1965), 16.

Bird, Donald E. "Teaching Listening Comprehension," **Journal of Communication,** 3 (1953), 127.

Broadbent, D. E. **Perception and Communication.** London: Pergamon Press, 1958.

Brown, Charles T. "Studies in Listening Comprehension," **Speech Monographs,** 26 (1959), 288.

————. "Three Studies of the Listening of Children," **Speech Monographs,** 32 (1965), 129.

Brown, James I. "The Measurement of Listening Ability," **School and Society,** 71 (1950), 69.

————. "The Objective Measurement of Listening Ability," **Journal of Communication,** 1 (1951), 44.

————. "The Construction of a Diagnostic Test of Listening Comprehension," **Journal of Experimental Education,** 18 (1955), 139.

————, and G. R. Carlsen. **Brown-Carlsen Listening Comprehension Test Manual.** New York: Harcourt Brace Jovanovich, 1953.

Caffrey, J. "Auding," **Review of Educational Research,** 25 (1955), 121.

————. "Auding Ability at the Secondary Level," **Education,** 75 (1955), 303.

Cardozo, Robert. "He Can Listen but He Won't," **Elementary English,** 40 (1963), 165.

Cartier, F. A. "Listenability and Human Interest," **Speech Monographs,** 22 (1955), 53.

Carver, M. E. Chap. 9 in Hadley Cantril and G. W. Allport, eds., **The Psychology of Radio.** New York: Harper and Row, 1935.

Chase, Stuart. **Roads to Agreement.** New York: Harper and Row, 1951.

Duker, Sam, and Charles R. Petrie, Jr. "What We Know About Listening: Continuation of a Controversy," **Journal of Communication,** 14 (1964), 245.

Erickson, A. G. "Can Listening Efficiency Be Improved?" **Journal of Communication,** 4 (1954), 128.

Faulkner, Leonard. "The Day the Clock Stood Still," **MONY Topics,** 3 (1963), 10.

Goldhaber, G. R., and Carl H. Weaver. "Listener Comprehension of Compressed Speech When the Difficulty, Rate of Presentation, and Sex of the Listener Are Varied," **Speech Monographs,** 35 (1968), 20.

Hampleman, R. S. "Comparison of Listening and Reading Comprehension Ability of Fourth and Sixth Grade Pupils," **Dissertation Abstracts,** 15 (1955), 1957.

Hanley, C. N. "A Factorial Analysis of Speech Perception," **Journal of Speech and Hearing Disorders,** 21 (1956), 76.

Heilman, Arthur W. "Critical Listening and the Educational Process," **Education,** 72 (1952), 481.

Horowitz, M. W. "Organizational Processes Underlying Differences Between Listening and Reading as a Function of Complexity of Material," **Journal of Communication,** 18 (1968), 37.

————, and Alan Berkowitz. "Listening and Reading, Speaking and Writing: An Experimental Investigation of Differential Acquisition and Reproduction of Memory," **Perceptual and Motor Skills,** 24 (1967), 207.

"Is Anybody Listening?" **Fortune,** 43 (1950), 77.

Johnson, Martha. "The Construction and Analysis of a Listening Test for the Intermediate Grades," unpublished dissertation, Ohio University, 1970.

————, and Don Richardson. "Listening Training in the Fundamentals of Speech Class," **The Speech Teacher,** 17 (1968), 293.

Kelly, Charles M. "Listening: Complex of Activities—and a Unitary Skill," **Speech Monographs,** 3 (1967), 455.

Kibler, Robert J., Larry L. Barker, and Donald J. Cegala. "Effect of Sex on Comprehension and Retention," **Speech Monographs,** 37 (1970), 287.

Knower, Franklin H., D. Phillips, and F. Koeppel. "Studies in Listening to Informative Speaking," **Journal of Abnormal and Social Psychology,** 40 (1945), 82.

Kristofferson, Alfred B. "Attention and Psychophysical Time" in A. Sanders, ed., **Attention and Performance.** Amsterdam: North-Holland, 1967, p. 93.

Leckart, B. T. "Looking Time: The Effects of Stimulus Complexity and Familiarity," **Perception and Psychophysics,** 1 (1966), 142.

Morton, J. "Interaction of Information in Word Recognition." **Psychological Review,** 76 (1969), 165.

Newman, John, and M. W. Horowitz. "Organizational Processes Underlying Differences Between Listening and Reading as a Function of Complexity of Material," paper read at the annual convention of the Speech Association of the Eastern States, 1964.

Nichols, Ralph G. "Factors in Listening Comprehension," **Speech Monographs,** 15 (1948), 154.

————. "The Teaching of Listening," **Chicago Schools Journal,** 30 (1949), 273.

————. "Ten Components of Effective Listening," **Journal of the National Association of Elementary School Principals,** 37 (1958), 21.

————, and L. A. Stevens. **Are you Listening?** New York: McGraw-Hill, 1957.

Orr, David B. "A Note on Thought as a Function of Reading and Listening Rates," **Perceptual and Motor Skills,** 19 (1964), 174.

Petrie, Charles R., Jr. "What We Don't Know About Listening," **Journal of Communication,** 14 (1964), 248.

Planty, Earl G., and William Machaver. "Stimulating Upward Communication" in M. Joseph Dooher and Vivienne Marquis, eds., **Effective Communication on the Job.** New York: American Management Association, 1956.

Rankin, P. T. "The Measurement of the Ability to Understand Spoken Language," **Dissertation Abstracts,** 12 (1926), 847.

————. "Listening Ability: Its Importance, Measurement and Development," **Chicago Schools Journal,** 12 (1930), 177.

Riesman, D. "The Oral and Written Traditions" in E. Carpenter and M. McLuhan, eds., **Explorations in Communication.** Boston: Beacon Press, 1960.

Rossiter, Charles M. "Chronological Age and Listening of Adult Students," **Adult Education Journal,** 21 (1970), 40.

Russell, David H. "Conspectus of Recent Research in Listening," **Elementary English,** 41 (1964), 262.

Sincoff, Michael Z. "The Development and Comprehension of Isolates of Meaning-Capacity and Their Application to Upward Directed Listening in Industry," unpublished thesis, University of Maryland, 1966.

Spearritt, Donald. **Listening Comprehension—A Factorial Analysis.** Melbourne: Australian Council for Educational Research, Series No. 76, 1962.

Sticht, Thomas G. "Some Relationships of Mental Aptitude, Reading Ability, and Listening Ability Using Normal and Time-Compressed Speech," **Journal of Communication,** 18 (1968), 243.

Vernon, P. E. "Investigations of the Intelligibility of Educational Broadcasts," British Association for the Advancement of Science, 1950. Cited in F. A. Cartier, "Listenability and Human Interest," **Speech Monographs,** 22 (1955), 53.

Weaver, Carl H., and W. L. Strausbaugh. **The Fundamentals of Speech Communication.** New York: American Book Company, 1964.

————, and Garry L. Weaver. "Information Theory and the Measurement of Meaning," **Speech Monographs,** 32 (1965), 435.

"Why Good Men Quit," **Changing Times,** 4 (December 1950).

Wilt, Miriam E. "A Study of Teacher Awareness of Listening as a Factor in Elementary Education," **Journal of Educational Research,** 43 (1950), 626.

Wright, E. L. "The Construction of a Test of Listening Comprehension for the Second, Third, and Fourth Grades," **Dissertation Abstracts,** 17 (1957), 2226.

TWO

Cognitive structuring: selective attention and data handling

Introduction

You cannot listen to anything without paying attention to it. This is a slight overstatement, but not much of one. In general, you are constantly operating in a process of selecting one stimulus from all the stimuli clamoring for your attention, handling that stimulus to your own satisfaction (either storing it for future use or making some overt response to it), and then turning to another. If you are not attending to external stimuli—that is, stimuli coming from outside yourself—you are attending to stimuli coming from within. Internal stimuli may come from internal sensors telling you the position or condition of your own body, or they may arise in the brain itself. In the latter case, you are doing some kind of thinking, perhaps daydreaming. As long as you are awake, however, your brain is never idle, and parts of it are active when you are asleep.

This process of selecting stimuli for attention is vital to listening. It is difficult to believe that you will understand anything about the listening process very well until you have developed some concept of the ways the human brain selects and processes data. Although the processes to be described in this chapter and the next are quite general—that is, they describe the way data are handled when they come in through any of the senses—you should constantly read as if we were talking only about aurally input data. The description has been written in that fashion, but it would be tiresome and boring to keep reminding you.

This chapter and Chapter 3 will not be easy reading. The processes described are complex, and you may see many words you have not seen before. At the end of this introduction some of them are listed and defined. Others are explained in the text itself. The definitions will allow you to develop a good enough concept for each term to enable you to understand adequately the processes involved when someone talks to you and you listen. It is hoped that an understanding of the process itself will help you to control it better, both as a listener and as a talker who wants someone else to listen.

It will help you to study carefully this diagram of the processes that take place when you listen:

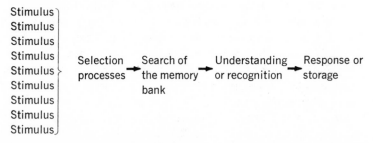

Let us assume that you are listening to a report made by a student in your class. At the same time, there are many messages being sent to you by all your senses—the sound of a motorcycle in the street, the shouts of students throwing a frisbee, the sound and sight of a wasp flying erratically behind the speaker's head, hunger pangs, the pressure of the chair against you, an itch on the sole of your foot, and many more. You cannot attend to all of them. You must select one or more to attend to. Whether you attend to the itch first or the chair pressure or to the speaker depends on many things. In general, although attention can be divided (as you will see later), you will attend to the stimuli in serial order, that is, one at a time. This means that as you attend to the itch your attention is diverted from the speaker. It means, too, that many incoming messages (stimuli) will go unattended, because they never cease and their numbers are constantly so great that you can attend only to those that have the greatest importance or value to you. Because of this, a selection process is constantly operating in your central nervous system, making it possible for you to attend to the most important messages and ignore those that do not matter much.

Once a stimulus has been selected, it is said to have your attention; that is, you become aware of it and "handle" it. Handling consists in instituting a search of all or part of the memory to find where the stimulus "fits." This will make more sense to you after you read the section of this chapter that explains concepts and categories. For the present, it is enough to know that each stimulus pattern has characteristics and that a search of part of the immense memory bank of the brain is instituted to find the area in which are stored memories of other stimuli with a similar pattern. The process is similar to a computer search, and, to be slightly facetious, it seems almost as if a little man is carrying a little template through the corridors of the brain, matching it to all the categories he passes until he finds one that it fits.

Once a match is made, you become aware of the "meaning" of the stimulus, because you know the meaning of the category in which it fits. This is true of unnamed sounds as well as categories of sounds for which you have names. In this book, however, in order to conserve words and time, most references to this process will concern categories with verbal names.

The selection and search processes are not affected by whether or not you make an overt response. You decide this after you have found or failed to find a match. Whether you respond overtly or merely store the data, you must give this response act your attention too.

At various points in this serial process, your behavior is colored by your orientation. Two of the most important variables in this coloring are discussed in Chapter 3: the sex of the listener and his biases. Both of these factors affect the stimulus selection and the handling of it after it has been selected. In short, they affect your listening— what you attend within a message and how you store it.

Definitions

You have read already some of these terms in this book and must already have developed some concepts for them.

> **Stimulus:** An electrical impulse sent along a string of neurons from a sensor to the central nervous system; thus the sound "pig" stimulates

the inner ear and sends an impulse along the eighth nerve. **Stimulus** also refers to the acoustical event itself.

Organism: Any living body.

Filter: This can be understood as a sieve or strainer. A better analogy is the electrical filter that passes some frequencies and not others, as in an electric organ.

Attenuate: To reduce the strength of something, as when you turn down the volume on your radio.

Inhibit: To prevent something from happening, to block its entry or its passage.

Orientation: Attitude or set.

Vigilance: Some degree of general arousal of the organism, the degree to which it is awake and alert.

Distraction method: A method of determining when an organism is overloaded. Usually it means that we give the subject two jobs to do and tell him by all means to do one well. The degree to which he can also do the other tells us what it takes to overload his data-handling system.

Attention energy, conservation of attention: An organism has only so much attention to use at any instant. This may be thought of as so much energy. Thus your attention will be keener if it is all devoted to one stimulus, less keen when it is divided.

Perceptual field: The entire area from which stimuli may arise. In the case of hearing, for example, it means whatever can be heard.

Scanning: Sweeping the perceptual field to discover what should be attended to.

Psychogalvanic responses: The basis for the lie detector. Under stress, certain parts of the body (hands, feet, temples) perspire, and an instrument can detect the perspiration. The greater the internal emotional response, the greater the perspiration.

Conditioning: Training by means of reward or punishment.

Threshold intensity: The lowest level of a sound (or other stimulus) that can be detected.

Switching time: The measurable amount of time for an organism to shift its attention from one stimulus to another.

Dwell time: The amount of time an organism must attend to an object before it can start switching. This simply means that although the period of time may be very short, it is a period of time. Dwell time apparently cannot be measured separately from switching time. The two are measured together.

Brain-stem reticular formation: An important part of the brain stem at the lower rear of the brain just above the spinal cord.

Exteroceptors: Sensors that are activated by external events—touch, taste, sight, hearing, and smell.

Interoceptors: Sensors that report the position or condition of the body, for example, the proprioceptors, which report the position and movement of muscles.

High- and low-value stimuli: These terms mean that at any instant some stimuli are more important to us than others. For example, the smell of food is not important after we have just finished eating a big dinner.

Interneuronal connections: The places where neurons, the long, wire-like extensions of nerve cells, are connected to each other; also called synapses, or joints. Neurons in the brain have many complex connections with other neurons.

Hypothalamus: A part of the midbrain lying about in the center of the head and believed to be the center of affect, or emotion.

Now let us turn our attention to **selective attention**, the process of selecting one stimulus from all the others.

Selective attention

"Everyone knows what attention is," wrote William James in 1890. And, indeed, attention was very important to great psychologists like James and Titchener because their theories were based on it. It was, however, part of the mentalistic psychologies and was investigated by the Wundtian methodology of introspection. When behaviorists like Watson denied the existence of any aspect of behavior that could not be counted, attention fell into disrepute. It was not until the orientation reflex gained the attention of the Russians and psychologists in England and America began to study vigilance that attention once again became a respectable field for study. Broadbent's great book (1958) probably began the revival, and scores of psychologists all over the world are now trying to discover how it is that of the myriad stimuli impinging on the organism from both exteroceptors and interoceptors the organism can select one—or only a few—and exclude the others from its concern.

There is no agreement yet on some parts of this question. Broadbent proposed a filter system through which all stimuli seeking the attention of the organism must pass, and Deutsch in part supported him.

But in the end Deutsch asserted that only the top command post, the cortex, could conceivably make some of the decisions Broadbent was assigning to his filter. Thus the neurological location of the filter—if there is one—is still in dispute. Treisman (1960) claims unselected stimuli are attenuated, that is, reduced in strength. Hernandez-Péon claims they are inhibited. Most investigators study attention as if only one stimulus can be attended at one time, but Vernon contends that what James and Titchener knew before the turn of the century is true —attention, though dissipated, can be directed to several stimuli at one time, and some stimuli that seem never to be attended nevertheless remain in the memory system and affect behavior.

Limits on what we can attend. Everyone has known for a long time that we cannot attend to everything. What has been called the "conservation of attention" (Sutherland and McIntosh) and "attention energy" (Weaver) has its limits. Although the orientation or vigilance level of the organism varies from instant to instant, no one would seriously contend that there is no limit. All laboratory studies reach it. Broadbent (1954) found, for example, that when he put different voices into the two ears of his subjects and directed them to listen to one, they were able to hear only a little of the other. Welford found evidence that the organism would delay attending to a signal until the previous signal had been disposed of. Moray (1959) found that listeners could always hear instructions in the preferred ear but could hear nothing of what came into the other ear unless their own names were spoken. Treisman and Geffen (1968) fed two messages to subjects, one in each ear. The subjects were asked to shadow (repeat aloud) the message in one (the preferred) ear and to tap with a ruler whenever a target word appeared in either ear. They tapped for 86.5 percent of the target words in the preferred ear, but only 8.1 percent in the other. Finally, many studies have been done by the distraction method—for example, asking subjects to do arithmetic problems while listening to a spoken message. In all cases like these, the limits of the attention energy are reached and subjects are unable to perform optimally beyond some limit.

Scanning illustrates this limit (Vernon). The organism can visually scan a perceptual field without really attending to any part of it, or it can stop and concentrate its attention on some part and perceive it clearly. There is some evidence that when a subject is listening to speech in one ear, he can periodically sample speech in the other, although not quite scan it. Moray (1959) has found that this occurs when the subject's name is spoken but not when only commands are issued. Vernon believes that we can, while scanning, estimate up to five or six items rather accurately but that beyond that we must fix attention on some part of the field scanned.

These studies demonstrate that there are limits to the number of stimuli we can attend at any given instant.

Handling data below the level of consciousness. Some evidence has been obtained in recent years suggesting that events of which the observer never becomes consciously aware may still influence his thoughts and actions. McGinnies's subjects demonstrated psychogalvanic responses to taboo words before they became aware of them and, in some cases, when they never did become aware of them. Lazarus and McCleary conditioned subjects to nonsense syllables with electric shock. Psychogalvanic responses occurred to these nonsense syllables before the subject could see on the screen what they were. Dixon obtained such responses to sexual words that were presented below threshold intensity and thus could not have been consciously attended. Similar effects have been secured by whispering a subject's name while he was asleep. This may occur without awakening him, or if he does awake, he may not remember the whispering of his name.

Vernon described an experiment in which road-safety propaganda posters were hung on the walls of a waiting room in which observers sat for three minutes before they went into another room to be tested. Some of these subjects were drivers and some were nondrivers. They had all been aware of the posters while waiting, but none seemed to remember them well. All were asked to look at photographs of accident scenes and point out errors they could see in regard to road safety. The drivers found significantly more errors than did the nondrivers. This was apparently not because of their driving experience. A control group of drivers who had not seen the pictures did no better on the task than did the nondrivers. Vernon called this "incidental learning." It has been well known in educational circles at least as far back as Herbart.

Time limits on attention. The amount of time devoted to one stimulus selected for attention may vary, of course, with its importance to the organism, the paucity of other high-value stimuli, and many other factors. It also takes time to shift from one stimulus to another. Vernon reported this time to be one-fifth of a second. Moray (1960) found his subjects able to shift four times per second if numbers were presented alternately to the ears with no overlap. This would be 250 milliseconds per item. But only 30 to 40 milliseconds of this time was needed to recognize the numbers. Thus the remainder of the time might be the time required for switching; but the switching time is confounded with what is called minimum dwell time—the time an organism must remain in a state before it can begin switching to another. The point is not important here. The point made thus far in this discussion is that the capacity of the organism to handle input data per unit of time is limited. Each percept takes time. We cannot attend everything. We can give complete attention to only one stimulus at once, and if we divide our attention, we divide some limited commodity. Ultimately, if we divide our attention enough, we are scanning. And when we scan we are only looking for something to attend, to become conscious of.

A center of attention. It has been believed for a long time that the brain-stem reticular formation has served as the center of attention (Vernon, perhaps Deutsch). **Life** in its Series on Man explained this as the center of all incoming data from exteroceptors and interoceptors, and suggested that it is here that low-value stimuli are shunted off into other circuits of the brain and high-value stimuli sent up to the cortex for attention. Broadbent (1958) posited this system and has been supported by others, although with some reservations.

Neural overloads. It is probably impossible to estimate how many inputs are available to the central nervous system at any instant. Miller has demonstrated that the human organism can handle about seven, although he did not mean that the organism can pay attention to all seven. What happens to the others? We have five **kinds** of exteroceptors; some of them—for example, touch—have tens of thousands of affectors, all of which might conceivably be activated at once. Obviously, sending all of these impulses to the cortex would constitute a tremendous overload, especially when the examination of some of them (the symbolic signals) must be handled as carefully as a later section of this chapter indicates. Some mechanism must be provided to protect the command post from such an inundation.

Deutsch (1963) developed an analogy that might explain in part the way the reticular formation could thus select the stimulus to be attended. If we could visualize stimuli as boys of various heights standing in a line waiting to be admitted to the full attention of the brain, then we could visualize the lowering of a level board until it touched the head of the tallest boy. This boy would then be passed upward to the cortex for attention. It is possible that two boys might have the same height and would both be passed at once. Indeed, this sometimes seems to happen.

Deutsch was not, of course, really talking about the height of boys but about the value—attention value or stimulus value—of pieces of input data. Different kinds of data are of varying degrees of value to an organism, and the values do not remain the same through time. Here Deutsch's model becomes a bit stickier, but it is not difficult to adapt it. As values of the organism vary—for example, hunger pangs become strong—the values of the stimuli change. Some of the boys that have been ignored all morning now become taller and are finally gated through. Why or how these changes are made no one seems to have any clear idea, but it is hard to deny that they do. It is possible that a better model than Deutsch's can be imagined that would really posit the reticular formation as a variable-biased filter, passing hunger pangs at one time but not at another. Connections between various parts of the reticular formation and almost every other part of the brain are very complex and very fast. It is not difficult to imagine that the reticular formation is constantly receiving directions as a result of decisions made in the higher centers, colored, as it were, by conditions throughout the system.

Neither is it difficult to imagine such delegations of authority. The brain stem, as well as other parts of the brain, already has such authority. The frequency and depth of breathing are controlled there, for example, and the frequency of the heart beat. Although the higher centers can intervene in the control of breathing and override impulses sent to the muscles, only in rarely known cases can it override control of the heart beat. We are talking here, of course, about somewhat mechanical processes. Decisions to increase the flow of blood or intake of oxygen result from chemical analyses of the blood and are not judgmental. It is when the decision reaches the level of judgment, as it were, that Deutsch and Treisman believe the decision is made in the cortex itself and the selective-filter function of the reticular formation is lost. That is, they believe the cortex does not delegate this kind of function to a lower center. Recognizing one's own name in an unattended channel is an example often used to prove that all input data is sent to the cortex and that the decisions are made there. This kind of decision is sometimes called **semantic,** and it is said that semantic centers are not located in the lower centers.

In addition, because of the known interneuronal connections between the reticular formation and other parts of the brain, including the hypothalamus, there is much reason to believe that the cortex does delegate to the brain stem the responsibility of protecting it from constant bombardment. Hernandez-Péon has demonstrated that in children of low intelligence and in adults where this function has been blocked by chemicals, attention is not possible and a condition of distraction exists.

Searching for a match to the stimulus pattern. It is believed that when an impulse pattern is thus selected by the filter and gated on to the cortex, a process of cognitive handling or structuring takes place. This takes a length of time that is often noticeable and sometimes measurable. A search is instituted for a match to the pattern, much as a computer searches for the code number of a registered college student in order to output his academic record. It is believed that elaborate systems of coding are used in order to avoid searching the astronomical numbers of patterns stored. The set searched thereby becomes smaller and the time and energy needed become possible. Noam Chomsky, a linguist, has suggested that kernel sentences may provide one such code. A question such as "Is the cat on the mat?" is stored as a kernel sentence with a code indicating the interrogative form. Thus it is remembered as "The cat is on the mat," plus the code. Such an arrangement would greatly facilitate the search process and speed it up, thus allowing the cortex to reach a decision and turn its attention to another impulse pattern. This complex process will seem even more useful—and necessary—after the reader has studied the description of ways in which the brain categorizes data.

Short- and long-term memory systems. Something should be said here about the so-called short-term and long-term memory systems. It is believed (Moray, 1960) that much input data decays and disappears within two seconds. This is probably what happens to the impulses that Hernandez-Péon believes are inhibited at the first sensory synapse. Other impulses reach the short-term memory system (STS) where they compete for attention. Most of these decay within thirty seconds. Some go through a process that neurologists call "rehearsal," which preserves them beyond the usual lifetime of the STS. No one is quite sure how these rehearsals take place, but it seems sure that some stimuli can be held in the STS until the cortex has time to attend them. It seems equally sure that some of them get into the long-term memory system (LTS) without ever having been attended, as Vernon has said.

Free will to choose what is attended. Finally, in addition to the decisions made in the brain about what is to be attended, the human organism can decide to attend to its own inner impulses or thoughts and ignore the outer world. This kind of decision is what we sometimes call **free will.** James wrote, "My experience is what I choose to attend to." MacDougall, another great psychologist, created what he called an "over-riding sentiment" to account for what seems to be complete freedom of the mind to choose what it will attend. It seems obvious now to psychologists, however, that even the so-called voluntary choice of what to attend is controlled by past experience and present condition. The cortex sends orders to the gating mechanism in the reticular formation because of what it has in itself, and what it has in itself has been recorded there in the past. This does not mean that MacDougall's over-riding sentiment has any more validity than it ever had. Man does become, as James has suggested, what he chooses to attend to, and what he chooses is determined by what he has chosen before. This idea deserves some careful attention. It comes about as close to explaining what we have always called free will as anything in the operation of the central nervous system does. When someone orders you to "pay attention and quit daydreaming," it may be possible for you to obey because the command becomes part of your present condition and causes the cortex to send orders down to the reticular formation. Thus the information or event you are ordered to attend is given higher priority in the selection process.

If you have read carefully the definitions given earlier in this chapter, you should by now have some idea of the process used by your central nervous system in the selection of stimuli for attention. You should realize that the brain is in constant danger of being overloaded by stimuli clamoring for its attention, and when you hear someone say that we can think four or five times faster than we can talk, you should begin to wonder whether such a statement is true or not. It may not be. Indeed, we cannot usually even hear everything that is said.

You should understand, too, that it is possible for you to divide your attention energy, a limited commodity, among several stimuli; but when you do, you can attend them less well than if you concentrate that energy on one stimulus alone. You should know that you can somehow remember stimuli which apparently you did not attend to, that the major attention center is in the reticular formation, and that most stimuli you do not attend disappear from your memory—in truth, they never get into it. Finally, you should consider the problem of free will and try to decide whether you can pay attention to something simply because you decide to and, if so, why.

The fluctuation of attention

You should not suppose that after you have selected a stimulus for attention, you can pay full attention to it as long as you like. The amount of attention energy you have at your disposal changes in accord with certain basic body rhythms, and when it wanes, your attention is sometimes very poor indeed, even though you are determined to listen to something as well as you can.

In 1739 David Hume wrote that an inkblot, when held at such a distance from the eye as to be barely visible, will periodically fade and become invisible. In 1875 Urbanschitsch, a German physiologist, described a similar phenomenon for auditory sensation. Both were describing the fluctuations of attention that have been studied since the turn of the century and for which a theory is only now being constructed. Scott timed such fluctuations and found some of them to be about six seconds in duration and others about twenty seconds. Pillsbury found cycles of about two seconds. Rohracher advanced the hypothesis that these fluctuations may stem from the alpha rhythms in the brain. Schmidt and Kristofferson also based their explanation of rhythm in the waxing and waning of attention (ranging from 63.8 to 66.4 milliseconds) on alpha rhythms.

It is well known that attention increases and decreases in intensity. You can demonstrate this for yourself by replicating the Hume procedure or by concentrating your attention with all your might on some barely audible but continuing sound such as the ticking of a clock. It can also be demonstrated by the "clothespin trick." It is easy to win a bet that a naive subject cannot hold a penny between the prongs of an old-fashioned clothespin for 60 seconds by squeezing the prongs together against it. The penny will slip out, not because of muscular fatigue, but because the bettor's attention has waned. In such a case, the bettor will usually testify that his fingers were not tired, and it is possible for you to speed up the process by talking to him or otherwise distracting him.

The phenomenon of fading attention is not, however, a product of distraction. Rather, it is a succession of lapses, actually kinds of very short sleep periods that Haider has called "microsleep." To demonstrate this phenomenon, Haider devised a technique of continuous measurements of sound-intensity thresholds along with simultaneous electroencephalograms of alpha waves. He had subjects press or lift a lever so as to keep the sensation of a continuous sound constant. Actually, the intensity of the sound **was** constant, but the cycling of attention made it seem to fluctuate, thus causing the subjects to press and lift the bar and activate a microswitch.

The picture of this action is represented in the dark recordings in Figure 1. The wavelike actions of the microswitch, resulting from the wavelike fluctuations of attention, can be clearly seen. Beneath the representations of the microswitch action can be seen the alpha-wave rhythms. In the second and third tracings, the periods of microsleep (the narrowest parts of the line) are longer because the subjects were tested during periods of sleep deprivation. In both of these tracings, reactivation of the alpha waves can be seen immediately prior to the reactivation of the microswitch. Haider believes the point of reactivation of attention occurs at the point where the alpha waves are activated; the lapse in time is only a motor delay. The tracings also show that deactivation of the alpha rhythm precedes deactivation of the microswitch.

This is supporting evidence from a laboratory of what was said in the first paragraph of this section: no matter how hard you try to attend to what someone is saying to you, you will miss some parts of the message periodically because you are, in effect, asleep. Determination alone will not overcome this problem. But, as you will see in Chapter 5, the talker can do something to help; he can help his listener listen.

Concepts and categories

In the first section of this chapter there was a paragraph about searching for a match to the stimulus pattern. The present section will explain in some detail what the search is for and what the match means when it is found. This explanation is very important to an understand-

Figure 1. Pictures showing the fluctuation of attention and periods of microsleep.

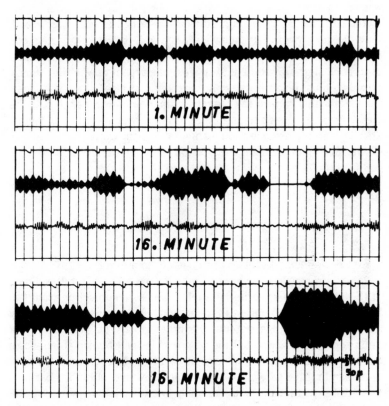

Reprinted by permission of Appleton-Century-Crofts from David Mostofsky, ed., **Attention: Contemporary Theory and Analysis**, 1970, p. 421.

ing of the process of listening to a verbal message because it will help you see how a listener gets meanings from the message, why it is that the meanings he gets differ somewhat from those the talker intends, and why he sometimes misses completely some of the things the talker says. Such an understanding should help you to listen better and also help you to talk in a way that will help your listener hear what you say.

In 1962 Bruner, Goodnow, and Austin published a book entitled **A Study of Thinking** in which they devised a system of categories to help them organize their data. Their system was probably the first important deviation from Aristotle's categorical definition system. It was found useful by Roger Brown and given wide dissemination in his **Words and Things.** Although **A Study of Thinking** has been much read, it was Roger Brown who made widely known this system of categories into which the mind sorts and assigns input data. The system will be used here, slightly modified, to suggest one aspect of what the human organism must do as it listens to a verbal message.

It is probably safe to say that the human organism cannot ascribe meaning to any input data until they have been assigned to a category. Then those data assume the meaning of the category.

The four kinds of categories. There are four basic kinds of categories, thus:

1. The single-attribute category
2. The disjunctive category
3. The relational category
4. The conjunctive category

We will define and explain each one of them in turn.

Categories have characteristics, which we will call **attributes.** Some of these attributes are criterial; that is, unless an object or event has them, it does not belong in that category. For example, the category named "fish" has one criterial attribute: gills. (The problem is not quite so simple as that, but the complexities will be explained later.) Such a category may be called a **single-attribute category.** This does not mean that the category—or the objects placed within it—has only one attribute. It means they have only one **criterial** attribute. Indeed, they have many others, but the others are not universal among the members of the category and/or they may not be confined to it. Most fish, for instance, have scales, but not all of them do.

The single-attribute category is a relatively simple one and easy to handle. The **disjunctive category** is more difficult. We place in this kind of category an object or event that possesses any one of two or more attributes. For example, a strike in baseball is called on the batter if a ball thrown by the pitcher has **any one** of these attributes: (1) the batter swings and misses; (2) the batter does not swing but the ball passes over the plate in the strike zone; (3) the batter fouls the ball off (although this attribute is criterial on only the first two strikes). When the pitched ball has one of these attributes, we assign it to the category named "strike."

The **relational category** is still more difficult. Into it we assign objects and events if they have certain **relational** attributes. For example, a triangle is assigned to this kind of category because of the relations among its parts. The equilateral triangle and the right-angle triangle have different relations among their parts and are assigned to kinds of categories with known attributes, and subsumed under the general relational category called "the triangle." When we assign a triangle to a subcategory and call it by the name of the subcategory (for example, "equilateral triangle"), we know what it is because we know the criterial attributes of the category.

The category named "father" is such a category, as are many others: cousin, grandfather, aunt, etc. The difficulty of handling such a category or concept may be seen in the difficulty a small child has in understanding the relation between his father and his grandfather. Usually he cannot understand this relation until he is several years old.

Finally, we use a kind of category called the **conjunctive category.** The criterial attributes required for assignment to this category are neither fixed nor stable in strength. We assign to it objects and events that have **enough of its criterial attributes in sufficient amount.** This is indeed flexible and causes many of our problems in listening.

Consider, for example, the expression "a good mother." "Mother," of course, has a single criterion for a biologist, but most people do not use it in the strictly biological sense. And when we append the adjective "good" to it, we are restricting it to a subcategory, the attributes of which are numerous and variable. To belong in the subcategory named "good mother," an object must of course have the attribute of the hierarchical category above it (named "mother"), but it must also have enough of the criterial attributes of the subcategory itself in sufficient amount. But what **are** the criterial attributes of a good mother? Perhaps we could divide them into two large classes: (1) those dealing with the physical and health needs of a child, and (2) those dealing with the psychological and support needs. It is easy to see that each of these classes contains long lists of attributes. Would we be willing to call a mother a good mother if she had only those attributes dealing with the health and physical needs of the child but none of the ones in class 2? Would we be willing to call her a good mother if she had all of those in class 2 but none of those in class 1? What about half of the attributes in each class? One-third? Obviously, very few mothers would have all the attributes in both classes—even if we could agree on the lists.

We could go through this routine with most of the terms we use that contain a value judgment. What is a good job? A good teacher? A good public speech? A good listener?

Subcategories. Every word in our language is used as the name of a category, whether it is a form-class word or a function word. When we hear a word spoken, it evokes the meaning of the category. If a word qualifies it, as "good" qualifies the word "mother," it simply evokes the meaning of a subcategory. Indeed, most categories are so complex that the single form-class or function word seems meaningless until a subcategory is specified by a modifier, which is itself part of the name of that subcategory. Sometimes, of course, the intended subcategory is established by the situation, or at least partly so, as when we hear a description of a fight between two men with knives. Yet there are many kinds of knives—pocket knives, switchblades, butcher knives, filleting knives, corn cutters, etc. The meaning the listener gets depends on which of his subcategories is evoked, and among many listeners these may be very different ones.

It is worth repeating that when a listener hears a word or a string of words spoken, he ascribes meaning to them because of the categories and subcategories evoked. This is a constant and very rapid process.

Noncriterial attributes. More may be said about the **meaning** evoked by words. In addition to its criterial attributes, a category (and the objects and events we assign to it) has many noncriterial attributes. Thus the word "Swede" is the name of a category with criterial attributes, but members of this category have other attributes. These attributes are not written or defined anywhere but are developed by every person individually from his actual and vicarious experiences. Perhaps one person has never known any Swedes but happy ones. Happiness is not a criterial attribute of the category "Swede," but a noncriterial one; nevertheless, part of the meaning of "Swede" to him is happiness. For every person there are many such attributes for every category that do not determine assignment to the category but are part of the meaning evoked when he hears the name of the category said.

Some of these attributes may be "noisy": that is, the person **thinks** they are criterial. Others may be "quiet," and never affect his assignment to categories. All contribute to the meaning of the category and of any object or event assigned to it.

Thus when we assign an object to a category, we "know what it is."

It takes on most of the attributes of the category. If we hear that a man is a paperhanger, for example, we know some things about him that we did not know before, because we know something about what paperhangers are—that is, we have a category with attributes. If he turns out to be an orthopedic surgeon instead, we change our minds and see in him the attributes of the category we have by that name.

How categories change. It is obvious that some of our attributes are erroneous. For example, some people have as an attribute of the category named "Swede" some characteristics that Swedes do not have any more than anyone else. Some people think that all Jews are shylocks and all students cheat on examinations. Because they are developed experientially, the attributes of a category are quite personal. It is doubtful whether any two people ever have exactly the same attributes for any category, especially the kind we call the conjunctive category.

Sometimes the criterial attributes of a category change, as when an error is made in its early formation and is corrected by later and more complete experience with the objects and events assigned to it. Certainly the noncriterial attributes are, in most cases and for most people, in a constant state of flux. As experiences broaden and knowledge increases, either directly or vicariously, old attributes die and new ones emerge. The meanings we have shift.

Sometimes, however, a person is so rigid in all or part of his conceptual life that his categories never change. Anything assigned to them is ascribed their attributes and even facts will not affect his perception of them. This has been called "the hardening of the categories" (Haney) and is what Walter Lippmann meant when he called the stereotype "a picture in the head." It is more common in uneducated people and in people who score high on tests of dogmatism.

How categories are developed. We establish most of our categories by experience. Hull has called this the "standard" method. Sometimes it is done in one experience with an object, as when Hull held a lighted candle before his little baby, who grasped the flame and was burned. Later, when Hull held a lighted lamp bulb up to his baby, the baby shrank from it. He had obviously, at that tender age, formed a category with two criterial attributes. He had, as Hull later called the process, abstracted at least one "common," or criterial, element and generalized from it. It is thus that we learn the criterial and noncriterial attributes of objects and events, assign them to one of the four kinds of categories, and **know what they mean.** From that time on, any object or event that contains what we believe to be the proper criterial attributes is assigned to that category. It means to us what the category means to us.

The first experience we have with a new term or word starts to establish such a category. A grandfather and grandmother were traveling through the West Virginia mountains with their four-year-old grandson. They stopped at a small grocery store on the top of a mountain to buy their grandson a Coke. He sat down in the dust to drink it. When he got up, his grandmother said, "Now, Grandpa, before he gets back into the car you must dust off the seat of his pants—firmly." The grandson, wanting to be cooperative, dusted off his own pants and then said, "There, Grampy, does that look firmly?" Obviously, the little boy had never heard the word "firmly," which was the name of a category, or concept, developed long before by both his grandparents. He had just heard it in context, however, and he had made a guess about its meaning. It was a poor guess—that is, his category was not at all like that of other people. No one knows when he discovered, by hearing the category name in other contexts, that the attributes were different from what he had thought. It is likely that the process was so slow and so incidental that the change was, though great, not noticed by him.

And so we learn. We learn names for concepts we have, and the names are words. It is not useful to learn words without concepts for them to name. The words slip away because we have no use for them. We develop categories with all their attributes through vicarious and direct experience, but they would not be useful to us without names, because we converse in names. The more we know, the more words we need, but the converse is not true.

How we use categories when we listen. We listen to names. Usually we hear not a single name, but a string of them. Consider this sentence.

The big red dog ran.

"Dog," of course, is a form-class word, and it is the name of a category. "Red" is the name of another category, as are "big" and "the." These three modifying names evoke in us a low-level subdivision of the general category named "dog." The meaning evoked in us is then the meaning (sum of the attributes) of the sub-sub-subcategory, not the general category named "dog." Of course, the object named has more attributes than those required by the category named "dog." There is some argument whether this indicates there is more or less meaning evoked by this phrase than would be evoked by the single word "dog." That is not important here. The important thing here is that a single subcategory is evoked by the entire phrase, and if a single one of the words is not heard, the wrong category will be attended to. The listener will miss the meaning.

The word "ran" is another category name, the name of an action, a category with its own criterial and noncriterial attributes. In our Indo-European language it is a necessary part of an utterance. It is possible —even quite likely—that the subcategory named by "the big red dog" and the category named by "ran" merge into one concept. At least the listener needs to identify both such categories to understand most messages.

Some laboratory studies of categorization. It should be noted here that the word "concept" has sometimes been used in this discussion synonymously with "category." And the word "meaning" has been used only slightly differently. Perhaps it will help in understanding the development of categories or concepts or meanings to describe a few of the early studies done to discover how it is that human beings develop concepts or categories.

Fisher, basing her work on that of several earlier workers, used the introspective (self-examination) techniques of Wundt, whose psychological laboratory is generally believed to have been the first in the world. She presented four kinds of geometric figures in groups of ten. Each kind (see Figure 2) had its own name—zalof, deral, tefoq, kareg—and its own criterial attribute, or feature common to its own group. As the figures were projected onto a screen, each with its own name printed below, five observers were instructed to "define the concept." That is, their task was to discover the common feature. These observers were skilled introspectionists and all of them held the doctorate in psychology.

They were asked to draw the feature of a figure common to all the figures with the same name. Afterward they were asked to describe the searching process as they remembered it. This was the process called introspection. They reported that quite early they found themselves ceasing to regard the figures as wholes. That is, those parts of the figures that were not repeated obviously could not be common fea-

Figure 2. Two examples of each of Fisher's concepts.

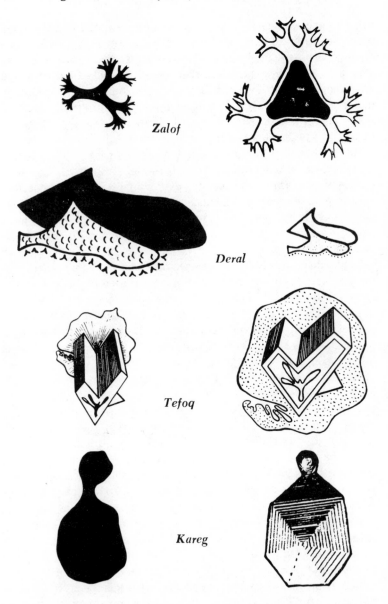

Zalof

Deral

Tefoq

Kareg

Reprinted by permission from S. C. Fisher, "The Process of Generalizing Abstraction; and its Product, the General Concept," **Psychological Monographs,** 21 (1916), 217–220.

tures, so they were ignored as irrelevant to the problem at hand. (This is a procedure used by listeners too.) They found also that they could draw the figure, including the criterial attribute, before they knew what the criterial attribute was. The **conscious** beginning of the abstraction process occurred when they made a decision "to investigate that feature." Perhaps the most important finding of this study is that the observers "knew" what the criterial attribute was some time before they knew that they knew.

This is true of many of our concepts, or categories, and has been demonstrated in many studies. It results in our often being unable to define a category or name its criterial atributes, even though we "know" it perfectly well and never err in assigning objects or events to it. Most people, for example, could not list the criterial attributes of the category named dog without including cats in it. Yet they never err in identifying cats and dogs. The point is that a considerable part of our category systems operates below the level of accessibility.

Hull set out to quantify some aspects of concept formation. He used a series of twelve Chinese characters, each with a common brush stroke that he called the concept but is here called the criterial attribute. In Figure 3 may be seen the single-syllable nonsense names and the common brush strokes. In series A, for example, the concept was named "oo," and the brush stroke stands beside it in the column labeled Concept. Every character in that horizontal line contains this brush stroke. Characters in all the other eleven lines in the table contain their own criterial attributes, or common elements.

The characters were arranged randomly on a revolving drum and an observer was seated before it, where he could see only one character at a time. He was not instructed to identify the criterial attribute— indeed, he did not know there was one. He was instructed only to learn the names of the characters as they appeared. He could not do this, of course, unless he **abstracted** from a series of characters this common feature and **generalized** it to all other characters containing this feature. This is exactly what we do and the way we go about it in real life, as a child, for example, begins to learn the categories named "horse," "dog," "cow."

The observer was shown the first character and asked to name it. He could not do this, of course, since he had not even seen or heard the list of names. After five seconds Hull named it for him, perhaps "oo" or "yer" or "li," then went on to the next character, which might

Figure 3. The concepts used by Hull, their nonsense-syllable names, and the characters in which they were embedded.

Reprinted by permission from C. L. Hull, "Quantitative Aspects of the Evolution of Concepts: An Experimental Study," **Psychological Monographs**, 28 (1920), 80.

be "ling" or "fid." In a surprisingly short time, Hull found his observers naming the characters correctly, at least part of the time. Even after they could name all of them without error, however, some could not tell him why. They had found the criterial attribute but below the level of accessibility.

Hull learned many things about the ways we learn concepts, and several of them are of interest to us here because they help to explain what happens when we listen. First, he found that learning is faster if simple configurations are presented before the observer sees the more complex patterns, apparently because the criterial attribute is easier to pick out. Second, he found that, at least with the subjects he used, forming concepts from concrete objects is not better than receiving them ready-made from an instructor. Third, the ability to define and draw the criterial attribute is better when the subject is told what it is than when he finds it for himself. Finally, a combination of being told and experience with the object is functionally the best way to learn a concept, that is, the criterial attributes of a category.

It will be useful to describe one more study about the ways we build concepts named by the words we use. Heidbreder used three kinds of concepts: concepts of concrete objects (face, building, tree), spatial forms (circle, the symbol for infinity, and #), and numerical quantities (two-ness, five-ness, and six-ness). All had nonsense names and were presented in random order as illustrated in Figure 4. The task of the observer was, as in Hull's study, to "learn the names" of the figures. Although the observer did not know it, it was necessary for him to abstract a common element from the group of figures and generalize to all figures with that element in order to name the figures properly.

Heidbreder found, as have many others, that her observers could name figures correctly some time before they could tell her why, indicating again that the generalized abstraction process occurs below the level of accessibility. She found also that names of concrete objects could be learned first, then spatial forms. Concepts of numbers presented the greatest difficulty, and Heidbreder concluded that for most people the perception of concrete objects is a dominant response.

Conceptualization is necessary for us to deal with our environment; if we can categorize many objects into a few categories, we need learn only a few reaction tendencies. We can treat many things alike, and

Figure 4. Figures used by Heidbreder in which the concepts were embedded. Shown are the first five of the sixteen series presented.

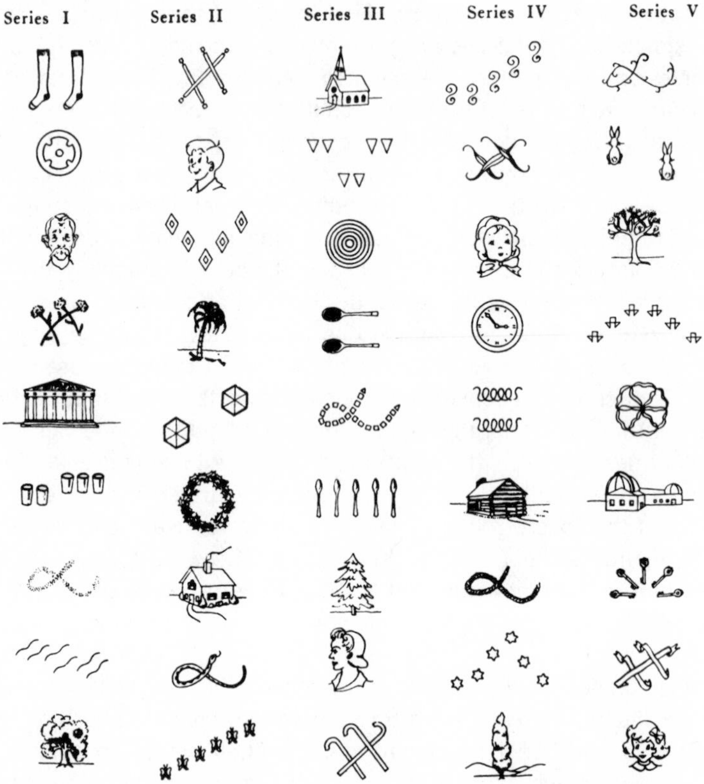

Reprinted by permission from E. Heidbreder, "The Attainment of Concepts. I. Terminology and Methodology," **Journal of General Psychology,** 35 (1946), 182.

when we hear people talk, we can understand what they mean by each word and phrase in the verbal message by finding the categories into which they fit. But the use of numbers is a clear departure from the perceptual situation. Numerosity (the concept of numbers) cannot be perceptually handled without the use of number symbols, which are not at all pictorial and are thus really not perceptual. We can actually perceive numerosity only up to about four or five, after which we must begin counting. A concept like counting is especially difficult for people who have a life style of dealing with concrete objects, and doubtless accounts for much of the criticism of the college lecture. Some people find almost any kind of verbal explanation difficult and would prefer the kind of learning that arises from manipulating their environment.

But listening consists in attending to verbal explanations. Except for what we might call "nonverbal listening," discussed in Chapter 1, concepts are evoked by their names, and the meaning attached because of the categorical attributes thus involved is the meaning the listener gets from the message. If he has no concept, or referent, for the word he hears, he can only guess. If his concept is lean, the meaning will be sparse. If he has no skill in handling nonconcrete categories, he may use so much time handling the data that he will miss succeeding parts of the message while he is working on the initial, puzzling problem. Finally, if most of the attributes of his categories are below the level of accessibility, he may not know why he gets the meaning he does get.

The complexity of our category structures. Something was said earlier in this discussion about the relative complexity of categorical organization. Indeed, the four kinds of categories are not so simple as the presentation here has made them seem. In the first place, a category may be formed on a formal or on a functional basis. This allows one concept to be stored in more than one category. A power lawn mower, for example, may be categorized according to its form or structure—it has four wheels, an engine, etc.—or according to its function. In the second place, as implied several times already in this discussion, categories are arrayed in hierarchies. Thus a power lawn mower is part of a larger hierarchy called "mowers," which would include hay mowers, reapers, etc. It is also part of a larger hierarchy called "tools" and probably of several other hierarchical systems as well. Thus any word may name a category that could—in the absence of further verbal specification—belong to several formal and functional hierarchical systems. The talker must indeed be careful to say what he thinks he is saying, but the burden on the listener is greater still. Not only must he be careful to hear the specification the talker actually does make, but also he must be continually guessing what the talker really should have specified. Not all talkers really say what they intend to say.

Lamb has illustrated this kind of hierarchical structure in connection with what he calls "stratificational grammar and structural correspondences between the formation of concepts and the neuron networks of the brain." This means that our language and systems of categories work as they do because that is the way the networks within the brain work. In Figure 5 is Lamb's stratification diagram of the game of baseball. It is, of course, a very simple and lean representation. Hundreds of other concepts could be represented in the figure, and a knowledgeable professional player could present a much more complex schema. It is shown here to illustrate the hierarchical complexity of our concept systems. You should realize that this is the way you understand verbal messages when you hear them and that there are many opportunities for error.

The search for a category to match the stimulus pattern. Pollack studied the time required for a human organism to decide which category a stimulus should be assigned to. He discovered that when the listener had many possible categories to consider, the time was greater than when the number of possible assignments was fewer. He used such categories and category members as these:

Name of category	Category members
Animal	Goat, pig, lion, leopard
Measure	Inch, rod, centimeter, gallon
Boy	Robert, Harold, Peter, Thomas
Tree	Spruce, oak, mahogany, elm

When arranged in this fashion, the problem for the listener seems simple indeed, but the listener in Pollack's experiment did not know this structure was the correct one. He had to guess from mention of the category members whether the name of the first category, for instance, was **animal, mammal, living organism, African wild game,** or some other name, and he had to guess it very fast, as we do when we listen. What Pollack found was that the greater the possible num-

Figure 5. A hierarchy of concepts.

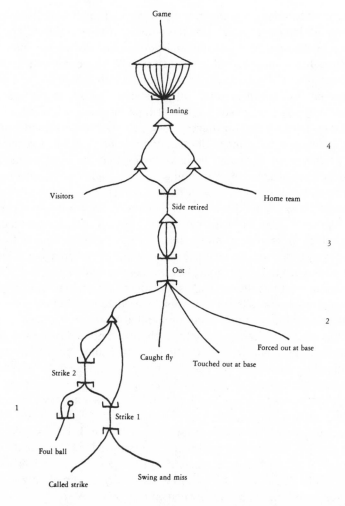

The game of baseball shown in a stratificational grammar diagram. In baseball there are three different types of strikes (1): the swing-and-miss; the called strike; and the foul ball. A foul ball can function only as a first or second strike. That is why there is no connection from foul ball to the third strike line. Likewise an out (2) may be reached in four ways: three strikes; a caught fly; touch-out at base; and force-out at base. Three outs retire a side (3), but both sides (visitors and home team) must be retired to complete an inning. Finally nine consecutive innings (4) make a game (unless there is a tie score at the end of the ninth inning).

Reprinted by permission from John White, "Language and the Brain," **Yale Alumni Magazine,** 47 (1969), 49.

ber of categories from which the listener had to choose, the greater the work load and the greater the amount of time required. And the list of categories here was formal. No functional system was included, although the listener had to expect one. When we consider that an object can usually be assigned to several different formal and several different functional hierarchical systems, it is easy to see that the listening organism needs some real time in which to search for the proper category or subcategory to which he may assign the input stimulus. And this time is limited. As he works, the talker goes on.

At this point, it should be easy to see that the human organism cannot pay attention to everything at once, and that in many cases, if not most, it can attend well to only one task at a time. One thing we do know about the brain is that only one **search** for category assignment goes on at a time. When a verbal pattern like "the big red dog" is heard, the mind starts its computerlike search for the category indicated. No meaning is evoked until that category is found. If the concept is commonly used or easily understood and if the listener is intelligent and sophisticated, the search may be very short. But if the opposite is true—that is, if the data are abstract, the category seldom used, the listener unintelligent and unpracticed in handling abstract concepts, the search may not end before another stimulus intrudes. Or if it continues, succeeding impulses may be denied the attention they need in order for the listener to understand them. The listener stands still while the talker goes on. Sometimes the listener cannot handle the data nearly as fast as they are spoken.

Sometimes the listener has no categories, as when a talker uses a strange word. The work load for the cortex then becomes greater as it searches a set for the most probable match to the pattern and makes a guess as to what its category might be like. When a talker uses a word like "exiguous," for example, to modify a form-class word, the listener may have no category named by it, and the wrong subcategory may thus be matched to the impulse pattern heard.

The searching process often requires so much time that the listener misses even common signals, as when someone may miss the word "red" in "the big red dog" and thus thinks of an English setter when the talker means an Irish setter. And when we add to this problem the cyclical character of attention, it is easy to see that the relatively slow rate of human speech may not be so much too slow after all.

In this section you have been reading about the way we categorize aurally input data when we listen. You may substitute the word "concept" for "category" if it is more meaningful to you. You should remember from your study of communication that words are symbols that name object referents and concept referents. We have been talking about concept referents, which are far more important in listening than object referents are.

You should understand that the four kinds of category—single-attribute, disjunctive, relational, and conjunctive—are **kinds** of categories. You have in your memory system thousands of categories of each kind. You should also keep in mind as you read and think about the listening process that you cannot understand—that is, assign any meaning to—a word or phrase until you find, as your brain searches, the category in which it fits. Then you know approximately what the talker means by it, assuming always that his category is about like yours. You should remember also that the search process takes time; that errors may be made; that your categorical structures are exceedingly complex; that the meaning you assign to a verbal stimulus results from noncriterial as well as criterial attributes; and that in most people these attributes change as their experiences change.

The attributes of a person's categories are the concept referents that are evoked in him as he listens to a verbal message. They are the source of the meanings he gets as he listens.

One final warning: our concepts are not the same, nor can they ever be. Most of them are formed, at least in large part, by our individual experiences. Their formation is affected by the two processes to be described in the next chapter.

Summary

In this chapter you have studied a description of some of the cognitive processes involved in listening, a rather technical but very important description of the process of selective attention, and evidence showing that attention will fluctuate in spite of any decision on a listener's part to pay attention well.

You have also read a description of the process of searching for a match to the stimulus pattern, which amounts to a search for a category with about the same attributes as that pattern. When the receiver knows the category, he is then able to ascribe meaning to the stimulus.

Your brain is a wonderfully complex instrument, and you must exercise all of its faculties when you listen. It is really rather marvelous that you can hear and understand as much as you do. But you can do it better.

Exercises

1. When you are trying to identify a sound, notice the time it takes.
2. Notice the time it takes for you to find a solution to a problem.
3. When you make a decision to study or to pay attention in class, ask yourself **why** you made the decision you did. Was it really a "free choice," or was it the result of what you are and want to become?
4. Try to define something by listing its criterial attributes. Then list some of its noncriterial attributes. Which of the attributes you have listed contribute most to its meaning for you?
5. Prepare a presentation to your class in which you take a sentence and point out how many categories (concepts) are represented in the sentence. Show how modifiers limit the concept to a subcategory of a larger category and how other modifiers may limit it still further. Then show how the meaning changes because of the modifiers.
6. Watch a sports announcer report the scores of basketball, football, or baseball games on television. He will probably roll the scores and names of the teams across the screen as he talks, and he will probably go so fast that you cannot quite handle the data. Try to work out a way to do it better; for example, try **seeing** the names of the teams and **listening** to the scores.

Bibliography

Ausubel, David P. "Meaningful Reception Learning and the Acquisition of Concepts" in Herbert J. Klausmeier and Chester W. Harris, eds., **Analysis of Concept Learning.** New York: Academic Press, 1966, p. 157.

Bakan, P., and B. T. Leckart. "Complexity Judgments of Photographs and Looking Time," **Perceptual and Motor Skills,** 21 (1965), 16.

Billings, M. "The Duration of Attention," **Psychological Review,** 21 (1914), 121.

Bourne, Lyle E., Jr., and Donald E. Guy. "Learning Conceptual Rules: II. The Role of Positive and Negative Instances," **Journal of Experimental Psychology,** 77 (1968), 488.

Broadbent, D. E. "The Role of Auditory Localization and Memory Span," **Journal of Experimental Psychology,** 47 (1954), 191.

————. **Perception and Communication.** London: Pergamon Press, 1958.

Brown, James I. "The Objective Measurement of Listening Ability," **Journal of Communication,** 1 (1951), 44.

————. "The Construction of a Diagnostic Test of Listening Comprehension," **Journal of Experimental Education,** 18 (1955), 139.

Brown, Roger. **Words and Things.** New York: Macmillan, 1958, Chaps. 3, 6, 7.

Bruner, Jerome S., Jacqueline J. Goodnow, and George A. Austin. **A Study of Thinking.** New York: John Wiley & Sons, 1956.

Caffrey, J. "Auding Ability at the Secondary Level," **Education,** 75 (1955), 303.

Cantril, Hadley, ed. **Tensions That Cause Wars.** Urbana, Ill.: University of Illinois Press, 1950.

Davis, R. "The Role of Attention in the Psychological Refractory Period," **Quarterly Journal of Experimental Psychology,** 11 (1959), 211.

Deutsch, J. A., and D. Deutsch. "Attention: Some Theoretical Considerations," **Psychological Review,** 70 (1963), 80.

Dixon, N. F. "The Effect of Subliminal Stimulation Upon Cognitive and Other Processes," unpublished dissertation, University of Reading. Cited in Magdalen D. Vernon, "Perception, Attention, and Consciousness," **Advancement of Science** (1960), p. 111.

Dow, Clyde W. "The Development of Listening Comprehension Tests for Michigan State College Freshmen," **Speech Monographs,** 20 (1953), 120.

Fisher, S. C. "The Process of Generalizing Abstraction; and its Product, the General Concept," **Psychological Monographs,** 21 (1916), 1.

Gray, G., and A. Wedderburn. "Grouping Strategies with Simultaneous Stimuli," **Quarterly Journal of Experimental Psychology,** 12 (1960), 180.

Haider, M. "Neuropsychology of Attention, Expectation, and Vigilance" in David I. Mostofsky, ed., **Attention: Contemporary Theory and Analysis.** New York: Appleton-Century-Crofts, 1970, p. 419.

Hampleman, R. S. "Comparison of Listening and Reading Comprehension Ability of Fourth and Sixth Grade Pupils," **Dissertation Abstracts,** 15 (1955), 1957.

Haney, W. V. **Communication: Patterns and Incidents.** Homewood, Ill.: Irwin Press, 1960, p. 12.

Hanfman, E., and J. Kasanin. "A Method for the Study of Concept Formation," **Journal of Psychology,** 3 (1937), 521.

Heidbreder, E. "The Attainment of Concepts: The Process," **Journal of Psychology,** 24 (1947), 93.

Heider, Fritz. **The Psychology of Interpersonal Relations.** New York: John Wiley & Sons, 1958.

Hernandez-Péon, Raul. "Attention, Sleep, Motivation, and Behavior" in Paul Bakan, ed., **Attention.** New York: D. Van Nostrand Company, 1966, p. 181.

Hollow, M. K. "Listening Comprehension at the Intermediate Grade Level," **Elementary School Journal,** 56 (1955), 158.

Horowitz, M. W., and A. Berkowitz. "Listening and Reading, Speaking and Writing: An Experimental Investigation of Differential Acquisition and Reproduction of Memory," **Perceptual and Motor Skills,** 24 (1967), 207.

Howarth, I., and K. Ellis. "The Relative Intelligibility Threshold for One's Own and Other People's Names," **Quarterly Journal of Experimental Psychology,** 13 (1961), 236.

Hull, C. L. "Quantitative Aspects of the Evolution of Concepts: An Experimental Study," **Psychological Monographs,** 28 (1920), 1.

Irvin, C. E. "An Analysis of Certain Aspects of a Listening Training Program Among College Freshmen at Michigan State College," **Journal of Communication,** 4 (1954), 42.

Ittelson, William H., and Hadley Cantril. **Perception: A Transactional Approach.** New York: Doubleday, 1954.

James, William. **Principles of Psychology,** vol. 1. New York: Holt, Rinehart & Winston, 1890, p. 402.

Jensen, Arthur J. "Individual Differences in Concept Learning" in Herbert J. Klausmeier and Chester W. Harris, eds., **Analyses of Concept Learning.** New York: Academic Press, 1966, p. 139.

Johnson, Wendell. "The Spoken Word and the Great Unsaid," **ETC.,** 11 (1953), 28.

Kelleher, Robert T. "Concept Formation in Chimpanzees," **Science,** 158 (1958), 777.

Kelley, Earl C. "Education Is Communication," **ETC.,** 12 (1955), 248.

Kimble, Gregory A., and Lawrence C. Perlmuter. "The Problem of Volition," **Psychological Review,** 77 (1970), 361.

King, W. H. "An Experimental Investigation into the Relative Merits of Listening and Reading Comprehension for Boys and Girls of Primary School Age," **British Journal of Educational Psychology,** 29 (1959), 42.

Lazarus, R. S., and R. A. McCleary. "Autonomic Discrimination Without Awareness: A Study of Subception," **Psychological Review,** 58 (1951), 113.

Leckart, B. T. "Looking Time: The Effects of Stimulus Complexity and Familiarity," **Perception and Psychophysics,** 1 (1966), 142.

———, K. R. Keeling, and P. Bakan. "The Effect of Rate of Presentation on Looking Time," **Perception and Psychophysics,** 1 (1966), 107.

Leeper, Robert. "Cognitive Processes," Chap. 19 in S. S. Stevens, ed., **Handbook of Experimental Psychology.** New York: John Wiley & Sons, 1951.

Lillywhite, Harold. "Toward a Philosophy of Communication," **Journal of Communication,** 2 (1952), 29.

Lindsley, D. B. "The Reticular Activating System and Perceptual Integration" in D. E. Sheer, ed., **Electrical Stimulation of the Brain.** Austin, Texas: University of Texas Press, 1961.

Looney, Nancy J., and Robert C. Haygood. "Effects of Number of Relevant Dimensions in Disjunctive Concept Learning," **Journal of Experimental Psychology,** 78 (1968), 169.

McGinnies, E. "Emotionality and Perceptual Defense," **Psychological Review,** 56 (1949), 244.

Miller, George A. "The Magical Number Seven, Plus or Minus 2: Some Limits on Our Capacity for Processing Information," **Psychological Review,** 63 (1956), 81.

Moray, N. "Attention in Dichotic Listening: Affective Cues and Influence of Instructions," **Quarterly Journal of Experimental Psychology,** 11 (1959), 56.

————. "Broadbent's Filter Theory: Postulate H and the Problem of Switching Time," **Quarterly Journal of Experimental Psychology,** 12 (1960), 214.

————. **Listening and Attention.** Baltimore: Penguin, 1969.

————, and T. Barnett. "Stimulus Presentation and Methods of Scoring in Short-Term Memory Experiments," **Acta Psychologie,** 24 (1965), 253.

Nichols, Ralph G. "Factors in Listening Comprehension," **Speech Monographs,** 15 (1948), 154.

————, and L. A. Stevens. **Are You Listening?** New York: McGraw-Hill, 1957.

Norman, D. A. "Acquisition and Retention in Short-Term Memory," **Journal of Experimental Psychology,** 72 (1966), 369.

————. "Memory While Shadowing," **Quarterly Journal of Experimental Psychology,** 21 (1969), 85.

————. **Memory and Attention, an Introduction to Human Information Processing.** New York: John Wiley & Sons, 1969.

Pillsbury, W. B. **Attention.** New York: Macmillan, 1908.

Pollack, Irwin. "Speed of Classification of Words into Superordinate Categories," **Journal of Verbal Learning and Verbal Behavior,** 2 (1963), 159.

Reik, Theodor. **Listening With the Third Ear.** New York: Farrar, Straus, and Giroux, 1949.

Rossiter, Charles M. "Rate-of-Presentation Effects on Recall of Facts and Ideas and on Generation of Inferences," **AV Communication Review,** 19 (1971), 287.

Savin, H. "On the Successive Perception of Simultaneous Stimuli," **Perception and Psychophysics,** 2 (1967), 479.

Schmidt, Marianne W., and Alfred B. Kristofferson. "Discrimination of Successiveness: A Test of a Model of Attention," **Science,** 139 (1963), 112.

Scott, Walter Dill. **The Psychology of Public Speaking.** Philadelphia: Pearson Brothers, 1906.

Spearritt, Donald. **Listening Comprehension—A Factorial Analysis.** Melbourne: Australian Council on Educational Research, Series No. 76, 1962.

Sperling, G. "The Information Available in Brief Visual Presentations," **Psychological Monographs,** 74, No. 498 (1960), 11.

Sutherland, N. S., and N. J. McIntosh. "Discrimination Learning: Non-Additivity of Cues," **Nature,** 201 (1964), 528.

Titchener, Edward Bradford. **Lectures on the Elementary Psychology of Feeling and Attention.** New York: Macmillan, 1908, p. 171.

Treisman, A. M. "Contextual Clues in Selective Listening," **Quarterly Journal of Experimental Psychology,** 12 (1960), 242.

———. "Verbal Cues, Language, and Meaning in Selective Attention," **American Journal of Psychology,** 77 (1964), 206.

———. "The Effect of Irrelevant Material on the Efficiency of Selective Listening," **American Journal of Psychology,** 77 (1964), 533.

———, and G. Geffen, "Selective Attention and Cerebral Dominance in Perceiving and Responding to Speech Messages," **Quarterly Journal of Experimental Psychology,** 20 (1968), 139.

———, and G. Geffen. "Selective Atttention: Perception or Response?" **Quarterly Journal of Experimental Psychology,** 19 (1967), 1.

Vernon, Magdalen D. "Perception, Attention, and Consciousness" in Paul Bakan, ed., **Attention.** New York: D. Van Nostrand Company, 1966, p. 37.

Vygotsky, L. S. **Thought and Language.** Eugenia Hanfman and Gertrude Vakar, trans. New York: John Wiley & Sons, 1962, Chaps. 5, 6, 7.

Wason, P. G. "The Processing of Positive and Negative Information," **Quarterly Journal of Experimental Psychology,** 11 (1959), 92.

Weaver, Carl H., and W. L. Strausbaugh. **The Fundamentals of Speech Communication.** New York: American Book Company, 1964.

Welford, A. T. "Evidence of a Single-Channel Decision Mechanism Limiting Performance in a Serial Reaction Task," **Quarterly Journal of Experimental Psychology,** 11 (1959), 193.

White, John. "Language and the Brain," **Yale Alumni Magazine** (December 1969), p. 47.

Wickes, Frances. **The Inner World of Choice.** New York: Harper and Row, 1963.

THREE

Cognitive structuring: two important variables

This chapter will discuss two important sources of pressure that affect the choices made by the brain as it selects and handles an aural stimulus. Both of them are also important to listening. They affect not only what you select to listen to but also what you do with it as you listen. The two sources of pressure are your biases and the fundamental and apparently innate differences between the sexes in the ways they perceive the world.

The pressures of bias

Everyone is biased—toward honesty or dishonesty, hard work or laziness, communism or dictatorship, and everything else man ever has contact with. Every concept we have has an emotional component in it; that is, we see it as unpleasant or pleasant. You can, by introspecting a little, see that this is true of you too. You can also probably find some concepts that contain both like and dislike; in this case, we say you are ambivalent.

This section concerns the operation of such biases in the process of selecting and handling aurally input data. They are very important to listening because they cause us to hear or not to hear different parts of a message. You can probably imagine, because you have studied in your history books about John L. Lewis, the great coal-mining labor leader, how differently the mine owners and the mine workers listened when Lewis spoke. They were battling over at least one scarce commodity—money—and they were strongly biased in opposite directions. There is no doubt that the two groups placed Lewis in different categories, and what he said meant quite different things as a result.

All of us listen in the midst of our own biases, and we will do it better if we are aware of them.

In this section you will read about the ways in which the brain alters the patterns of incoming data, the effects of your biases on your thinking, and the effects of evaluating too soon, before you have heard the entire message.

The alteration of incoming data. When Brown (1951) was constructing the Brown-Carlsen Listening Comprehension Test, he tried out his test items on many people. He found one strongly opinionated young man who marked a test after he heard a lecture exactly the same way he had marked it before he heard the lecture. This led Brown to construct a strength-of-opinion subtest, in which he asked his listeners to rate some statements on an agree–disagree scale. He found that some people consistently marked the extreme ends of the scale —indicating they held their opinions very strongly—and that others consistently marked the "undecided area." Both of these kinds of listeners scored less well than others on Brown's listening-test items. Primarily, they tended to miss the inference items and the items that tested their knowledge of the general idea of the lecture. So consistent was this effect that Brown decided that either of these two kinds of inner state of the listener would affect his listening capacity.

It will help you in understanding how your brain alters the messages you hear to read about some of the studies that have demonstrated this process in others.

Feshback and Singer conducted a test in which they created fear in their subjects by shocking them with a mild electrical charge while they were watching a movie of a young man performing some ordinary tasks. Half of them were told to go ahead and express their fear of the shock and the other half were told to keep still about it, to "suppress" it. After the movie, they were asked to describe the personality of the young man. Those who were not allowed to express their own fear of the oncoming electric shock while viewing the movie projected the fear onto the actor in the movie. The others did so much less. Apparently, retaining the negative affect, or emotion, in the system allowed it to have a significant effect on what was perceived.

We tend to turn off what we do not want or cannot bear to hear. Wispé and Drambarean showed this effect rather dramatically by starving their experimental subjects. First they established base lines of recognition for a series of twelve food-and-drink (need) words for each subject, along with twelve neutral, non-need words to establish a control. Then the subjects went without food and drink for twenty-four hours. At the end of ten hours, they were tested again for their speed of recognition of the need words (six food words and six drink words). This time they could recognize the words much more quickly as they were flashed on the screen for only some hundredths of a second. They went on fasting and were tested again at the end of the twenty-four hours. Now they would hardly see the words at all. In a few cases, a word had to be shown for almost a full second before the observing subject could (or would) recognize it.

It is obvious what was happening at the end of ten hours of fasting. The subjects had such great need for food and drink that they could perceive words related to that need very quickly. The organism perceives well what it needs and must perceive. At the end of twenty-four hours, however, the tension within the subjects was too high to be tolerated. They could avoid pain only by avoiding attention to the need, and though they could not avoid looking at the screen, they could suppress or repress what they saw there. Wispé reported that they behaved as if there were a little man in the cortex resolutely closing the gate on all perceptions that could arouse intolerably high tensions.

During all these tests the threshold recognition of the twelve neutral, non-need words remained the same. Thresholds were affected only in the area of need.

It was long believed—and probably still is in some quarters—that the organism receiving input data is only a receiver; that is, it sees the world as it is and all like organisms see it the same way. Instead, we make the world what we must make it and what we need to make it. It is probably a mistake to say that we can make it what we choose. We must choose what we need.

Harry Stack Sullivan developed this thesis extensively in his theories of patient treatment. He believed that a child quickly learns to discriminate increasing from decreasing anxiety and to alter his behavior so as to keep himself out of anxiety-producing situations. He learns to ". . . chart a course by the anxiety gradient. . . . Before he is very many months of age, the child will be showing full-fledged sublimation in the sense of quite unwittingly having adopted some pattern in the partial, and somewhat incomplete, satisfaction of a need which avoids anxiety." The inducing of anxiety is a very special form of punishment and may quickly assume intolerable levels. The organism avoids it by not hearing or seeing what produces it.

We filter the outside world in by a "curious engineering scheme." If necessary, we will partially or wholly exclude perceptions that we cannot or do not want to hear. And the opposite is true also, as Wispé and Drambarean demonstrated: we will hear easily and quickly those things we need and want.

Since most characteristic needs and wants of an organism do not usually change overnight, we develop what Heider has called "perceptual constancy." We tend, day after day, to perceive the world in about the same ways; that is, the incoming data are selected that fit and support our internal frame of reference. Our perceptual style causes us to hear consistently about the same kinds of data and to reject without attending other kinds. Thus we become, as we grow older, more and more like ourselves, stereotyping, overestimating and underestimating, confusing the figure and the ground more and more consistently, making about the same errors, and misperceiving because of a more and more rigid internal frame of reference.

So strong is this tendency that Bernberg has made what he calls a "direction of perception" test. He constructed items that had no foundation in fact, answers for which were based on the respondent's perception of some part of his world. Here is one item:

> It has been found that in groups such as yours most workers:
> a. Do what is required.
> b. Do more than is required.

The respondent was forced to choose (a) or (b) and his answers revealed the way he perceived the world. He would choose answers in the direction of his bias. The test showed highly significant and consistent differences among people in an aircraft factory.

Kelly found that "good listeners"—that is, listeners who scored well on his tests—were adventurous, emotionally stable, mature, and sophisticated. "Poor listeners"—those who scored low—were timid, tense, emotional, and simple. These characteristics suggest that Kelly's good listeners had fewer strong internal biases affecting their reception of the message.

The effect of bias on thinking. The strength of internal biases affects our thinking and our evaluation of the messages we hear. Several early studies demonstrated this well. Morgan and Morton constructed a test of two kinds of syllogisms. One was concerned with attitudes toward the Japanese, and the other concerned letters of the alphabet in the following way:

Major premise: No A's are B's.
Minor premise: Some C's are B's.

His subjects were asked to select from six conclusions the one that logically followed from the two premises, in this case, "No logical conclusion can be drawn from the given statements." They could do this very well, indicating that their command of syllogistic reasoning was adequate, but when the items concerned the Japanese, they consistently chose the conclusions in line with their own beliefs. Here is an example:

Major premise: A trustworthy man does not engage in
        deceitful acts.
Minor premise: The bombing of Pearl Harbor by the Japanese
        was a deceitful act.
Conclusions: 1. All of the Japanese are trustworthy.
        2. Some of the Japanese are trustworthy.
        3. Only a few Japanese are trustworthy.
        4. Some of the Japanese are not trustworthy.
        5. Most of the Japanese are not trustworthy.
        6. None of the Japanese are trustworthy.
        7. No logical conclusion can be drawn from
        the given statements.

In this case, the logical conclusion was number 4, but subjects overwhelmingly marked number 6.

Gilbert set out to teach high school science students "to think better" by teaching them logic. He administered a "prejudice test," which showed that some of his students were more highly prejudiced on the subjects of his syllogisms than others. But when he had finished teaching them to think better and then administered his test, which was similar to Morgan and Morton's, he found that all of them, biased or unbiased, chose the conclusions they wanted and not those that followed logically from the premises. This suggests that the tendency discussed here is probably universal. All of us do it.

Conclusions are inferences. Inferences are meanings we get from something said, but the inferences we make are not said by the talker. They are supplied by the listener. (This was discussed in Chapter 1.) It is easy to see that the inferences made by various people depend in some large part on their direction of perception, which is in turn dependent on their internal biases. It is probably true that we can hardly understand the intended meaning of any utterance without making an inference about the intention of the talker. It is likely that the most important part of our communication is the part we infer. And yet we do this through our screen of personal biases, our needs, and our affective states.

Premature evaluation. Finally, Rogers has suggested that all of us have a very human tendency to evaluate too soon what we hear. The evaluation, of course, fits our own frames of reference and our needs. Furthermore, once we have made such an evaluation, it strongly affects what we hear afterward. We select for attention what fits the evaluation and reject what does not. Rare is the good listener who can get the talker's story before he begins to accept or reject it.

In this section you have read a brief discussion that should convince you that what you hear is not necessarily what the talker said, nor is it likely to be all he said. Your biases cause you to hear what you want and need to hear and ignore the rest of the message. Your listening may become better to the extent that you are aware of your own biases. When you become aware of them, you can control them better and hear more of the message.

Sex and listening

The great majority of studies in listening have reported no differences between the sexes in postlistening test scores. Others have, however, reported such differences. Hampleman,* in a study comparing listening and reading comprehension abilities of 4th, 5th, and 6th graders, found that male subjects scored significantly higher than females on his listening tests. Hollow* found the same effect in 5th-grade

* See Bibliography for Chapter 2.

pupils. King* found it in grade 6 in England. Caffrey* found it in grades 9 through 12. Dow,* Irvin,* and Nichols* found it in college freshmen in Michigan and Wisconsin. Goldhaber and Weaver found it in college students at the University of Maryland. Such a variety of locations and levels seems convincing enough to have stirred speculation and research, but it has not, probably because the majority of studies have found no differences between the sexes, and because the studies cited above have been considered the products of aberrant populations. Weaver, for example, found no differences between scores made on achievement tests by men and women in a large intercollegiate listening contest. However, no study has been discovered in which females scored higher than males on achievement tests administered after listening. We should not assume that these results prove that one sex listens better than the other.

The words "scored significantly higher" should be understood before continuing. A higher score does not necessarily mean a "better" score. A high score on a test of neurotic tendencies, for example, is "worse" than a low score, and a high score on an attitude test usually means simply that the respondent has a more favorable attitude toward something than someone who produces a low score. The attitude object may be whisky, motherhood, war, sizzling steaks, or God. In such cases, "high" scores reflect only **differences** among people, not goodness or badness. In like manner, scores on listening tests may reflect only **differences** between the sexes and not the quality of the listening at all. If it is true that women hear one kind of data "better" than men do, and men hear another kind "better" than women do, it could be shown that people of either sex are "better" listeners if the experimenter uses the "right" kind of test, or even the "right" kind of material for them to listen to.

It would be naive to claim that there are no psychological differences between females and males. Many differences have been shown, and as far as the processes involved in listening are concerned it matters not at all whether the differences are innate or socially developmental. Furthermore, researchers are loath to evaluate such differences and label one sex better that the other. When the reader of such reports places such a label on them, it is the reader who does so, and not the scientist. For example, the characteristic called "toughmindedness," a term coined by the great psychologist MacDougall,

* See Bibliography for Chapter 2.

means the willingness of a person to abandon old and cherished beliefs when new evidence is discovered which discredits them. Whether tough-mindedness is good or bad does not concern the scientist who does the research, and it would be a mistake to blame him for the existence of some truth his research has unearthed. This has been done, of course, in many well-known instances: Darwin was criticized for his discovery of the process of evolution; Lindbergh was reviled when he reported in the United States the strength of Hitler's armies; even the great poet Walt Whitman was ostracized when his **Leaves of Grass** was published.

This section will review some of the differences between males and females, as established and now well known, **in the ways they select data from their environment and attend it.** Since the material to be reported here is not generally well known by communication scholars and since in these days of Women's Liberation some people are reluctant to believe that women are psychologically different from men, at least some of the supporting evidence will be presented. (Much more is listed in the reading list at the end of this chapter.) Afterward, since listening must almost inevitably be affected by ways in which data are selected and handled, the question of why sex differences which appear in the studies to be cited below have only occasionally appeared in tests of listening will be considered. You should avoid inferring that experimental results which show that differences exist between the sexes imply any evaluation of the differences.

Male and female attentional styles. Silverman has collected evidence that demonstrates many differences between the sexes in the way selective attention operates. He posits two kinds of attentional style, one of which is the typical feminine style and the other the typical masculine style. They are patterned after the principles of Jung and Wickes, and behavioral evidence of them has been demonstrated in the ways that people, from infancy onward, **select stimuli to pay attention to** and in the ways they handle data after they have been selected. You should remember that we are not now considering the process of listening but of data selection and handling.

We will first describe the attentional styles themselves, and then some of the research that seems to have demonstrated their validity. The male attentional style refers to the so-called analytic mind that is "continually shaping, forming, observing, inquiring, and directing

energy toward a chosen goal, a new structure." The male style is "objective, active, tough-minded, analytic, rational, unyielding, counteracting, intrusive, independent, self-sufficient, emotionally controlled." The female attentional style describes the mind that searches for "relatedness of parts of a pattern, of intuitive perceptions of feeling situations, of openness of images of the unconsciousness as well as to the external environment." The female attentional pattern is one of subjectivity, passivity, tender-mindedness, diffuseness, sensitivity, impressionism, yielding, receptiveness, empathy, dependency, and emotion. The female is more easily distracted by competing details, whereas the male finds segments of configurations (criterial attributes) and ignores much of the message that the female hears quite well. The male is less aware of subtle differences between parts of a configuration because he ignores most parts. He tends to restructure the configuration in the light of his goal, whereas the female tends to accept the pattern as it is in order to perceive relations, including social relations. This would tend to allow the female to hear more of the data in a message because she rejects less of it. It would also tend to cause the male to make more coherent sense of a message—that is, hear more general ideas and conclusions—because building general structure is his main interest as he selects and handles input data. Finally, the female attentional style allows emotions and unclear impressions to govern selective attention more than the male. All these differences would allow male and female listeners to select quite different segments of any kind of stimulus and respond to them in quite different ways.

Evidence of these differences between the sexes begins with newborn babies. The readiness to register and experience sensory input is quite different for baby boys and girls from the first day after birth. In general, males at this age tend to show less sensitivity and lower arousal levels than females. They are also more readily able to respond to configurations that are easily segmentalized than are female babies; that is, they will respond to parts of the whole, whereas females will respond to complex forms that are less amenable to critical analysis (Bell). Lewis et al., demonstrated this at the age of six months, using jazz music and intermittent tones and simple and complex verbal stimuli. Having previously demonstrated that a slowing of the heartbeat is an indicator of attention, they used this as an index to discover that the male babies consistently attended the stimulus configuration of minimal complexity, whereas the females attended the complex patterns. They could tell by a slowing of the heartbeat when the baby was paying attention.

Taylor and Eisenman found the same effect in college-age males and females. Females have been found to be more yielding in persuasibility experiments (Janis et al.), more conforming (Belof), and more highly suggestible (Patel and Gordon). Females consistently score higher than males on tests of perceived relatedness, such as the similarity subtest of the Wechsler Adult Intelligence Scale. But in problem-solving tests, females tend to be influenced more by distracting parts of the configuration. A good example of this tendency is that on Witkin's rod-and-frame test females tend to be influenced more than men in their judgment of the verticality of the rod by the tilted background frame. (The rod-and-frame test is a rather simple picture of what might be called a window frame. Inside the frame is a rod. The rod and frame are both presented in various degrees of verticality or uprightness. Observers are then asked to judge the verticality of the rod. Their judgments are influenced by the position of the frame.) Females cannot restructure the relevant aspects of a problem as completely as males (Guetzkow). Females do less well than males on tests of space visualization in which restructuring is necessary, and in perceptual-judgment tests in which the influence of some stimulus segments must be handled as separate parts of the configuration. But they exceed males in their ability to attend to details. They also exceed males in their ability to detect subtle cues of relatedness.

All this tends to support the existence of the two attentional styles, and the evidence presented here is only a small part of the evidence represented in the relatively few reports in the reading list at the end of this chapter. The studies cited here were selected to show that the two attentional styles have been well documented in most, if not all, of their dimensions, from the very first day of life through adulthood.

There is much overlapping of the sexes in these styles. Males who score high on femininity traits tend to select stimuli for attention as females do. Females who score high on masculinity factors have been said to be using a masculine pattern of selective attention and handling of data. For example, females who score as well as men on the rod-and-frame test also score like men on the Terman-Miles Masculinity-Femininity Test (Silverman). Vaught also found that females who scored high on the rod-and-frame test scored like men on the

Barron Ego Strength Scale; that is, they produced high ego-strength scores and low femininity scores.

In summary, these attentional styles are regarded as prototypes for the two sexes in the matter of the selection and handling of input data from any of the sense modes.

The effect of attentional styles on listening. Although the tendency to find that males at many educational levels surpass females in scores on listening tests has been labeled by Spearritt "persistent," it is not. As noted earlier, reports of this tendency have been in the minority, so much so that one researcher who found differences between the sexes was reluctant to publish his results. In the light of the evidence just reviewed about the fundamental differences between the sexes in **attentional styles,** one would expect reported differences on **listening-test scores** to be more numerous than they have been. This is because attention and data selection are so integral to listening, just as they are integral to data input processes for any of the senses. No data can reach the central nervous system and be handled —even from within the organism itself—without first having been selected and attended. If the two sex-related attentional styles have any validity—as the research evidence seems to demonstrate—we must expect data input via the auditory mode to be affected by them. It will be worthwhile to consider, in light of what we know about listening training and testing, the question of why in some studies males scored higher, why some showed no differences between the two sexes, and why none have been reported in which females scored higher than males.

There may be several reasons for this failure to demonstrate at the relatively gross level of listening what has been demonstrated so well at a neurological level. One possibility is that too little attention has been paid to the confounding of the interest level of the material listened to and the motivation of the listeners. Some researchers have controlled, at least to some degree, the interestingness of the material (Caffrey,* Rossiter*). Others have apparently ignored the question or have not reported any controls. Rossiter, for example, used fourteen one-and-a-half-minute messages on a variety of subjects, but he made no effort to find out whether this procedure equalized the interest level of males and females. That is, he did not ask men and

* See Bibliography for Chapter 2.

women how interesting they thought each selection was. Dow apparently did not control this factor at all. And no controls are reported for the Brown-Carlsen Listening Comprehension Test or for the Xerox pretest and posttest.

It has been demonstrated that if the motivation of the listeners is high, the interestingness of the message will not affect scores on the test taken afterward; that is, if listeners are motivated, they will listen to a dull passage as well as to an interesting one (Spearritt). When motivation is less than optimal, it may be that the interestingness of the message will affect the scores of one sex more than those of the other and produce a result that is actually an artifact of the testing situation. This may have been the case in the study done by Goldhaber and Weaver, where three messages were used—one on the structure and functioning of television cameras, one on the history of television, and one from a novel. The males and females may have been equally interested in the novel, but it is possible that the males were more interested in the two selections on television than the females were. If motivation was not maximized—and who ever knows whether it is or not?—the interestingness bias may have caused the males to score higher on the tests.

Two other possible problems may be presented as reasons why the two fairly clear attentional styles have not usually produced consistent differences between the sexes in scores on listening tests. First, few researchers are sophisticated in the making and analyzing of tests. Probably not more than half a dozen (including Brown, Rossiter, Goldhaber, Spearritt, and M. Johnson) analyzed and revised their tests. Most of the listening tests reported have been made simply by composing some kind of question with an answer that appeared in the material heard. The test-maker seems, at least in his report of the study, simply to have assumed that his test was measuring reliably what he thought it was. Thus we have little idea when we read his report whether his test was measuring anything well.

The second testing problem concerns what a reliable achievement test measures—that is, its validity. It is obvious that even if a test does have adequate reliability, even if every item does discriminate between good and poor listeners, and even if the difficulty of the items is distributed evenly across the message, it could still be a test that measures what the male attentional style causes the listener to select and attend. Such a test would, of course, cause males to score higher.

Rossiter's test seems to have avoided this problem. For each of his fourteen short messages he prepared two test items that asked for knowledge of details, two that asked for knowledge of general ideas, and two that asked for inferences made from explicit data. Male and female attentional styles would apparently generate about equal scores on such a test, and they did. Weaver's test in the intercollegiate listening contest asked for details only, which would give females an advantage. Lack of difference between the sexes on this test might have been caused in part by the exceedingly high motivation of the contest situation. But it should be remembered that details are of varying levels of abstraction. Some items asking for memory of details may also be good fits of the male attentional style. It is quite possible, and quite likely, that, in the eight studies cited at the beginning of this section which reported that males scored higher than females on listening tests, the tests were constructed so as to favor the male attentional style. Other tests might have generated higher scores for females, or for neither.

It is likely that no one will ever conclude that either sex can listen better than the other; they only listen differently. From what we know about basic differences between them in their **attentional styles,** we should expect them to **hear different data,** but "superiority" will appear only as a result of what we test and, perhaps, of what the subjects are given to hear.

You have been reading in this section about several basic differences between men and women in the ways they select input data. This probably applies to listening as well as to the other senses. You should realize that as a result of these differences men are not going to hear the same meanings when you talk as women will. Women will probably hear the details better and the social relational data. They may not fit what you say into what they already know as well as men will. They may be more emotional and more easily persuaded and will probably select data on the basis of humanistic values more than men will. In short, they will hear different data in your message. But that does not make men poor listeners, nor does it make women poor listeners. It only makes them somewhat different. You should realize this and correct your talking for it as much as you can. You should remember that, although the hypotheses concerning attentional styles have been quite well substantiated, their effects on listening have not. The presentation of these studies has been made here because of the close, and apparently causal, relation between the selection and handling of input data and the process of listening. If the carburetor on your car has been adjusted, your car will run differently. So do the cognitive operations of the human organism depend on its mechanisms of data input.

Summary

In this chapter you have learned how two variables affect the cognitive processes described in Chapter 2. First, you learned how your own internal states and attitudes may cause you to select and handle those parts of the data which fit your needs and knowledge and to neglect the rest of the message. Second, you read some of the evidence that men and women are really different in the ways they select and handle stimuli.

After having read this chapter, you may have lost some confidence in your ability to hear exactly what is said to you. You should. Your own inner states make it difficult to hear anything above the level of the most simple messages. You will have to become aware of your biases and do what you can to control them in order to become a better listener.

Exercises

1. Write a short **behavioral** description of someone. Do not write what he is like but some little things he does, like this:

   "Jim took a cookie out of his lunch pail on the way to work and ate it as he walked along the sidewalk. Before he had finished it, a scrawny dog came up to him and looked at him hungrily. Jim gave the remainder of his cookie to the dog and walked on to work. When he got there, he set his lunch pail down on the floor beside his lathe and turned on the switch."

   Read your description once to several friends and ask them to write an answer to this question. What kind of fellow is Jim?

   Afterward, ask them to underline on their papers everything they wrote about Jim that was not explicitly stated in the story. Then read the story aloud several times and ask them to check their underlining. What they have underlined is probably a number of inferences, and they will not be alike from person to person. Get the group to discuss them. Can they discover any reasons why the inference should not be the same for everybody?

Do not let them get away with the loose statement that "everybody is different."

2. Find a couple of factual statements in a newspaper about something that is highly controversial. Find two people who have extreme opinions in opposite directions on the subject and ask them to interpret the facts you have found.

3. When someone talks to you and you find yourself resisting what he says, try to discover the reasons for your resistance. Could it be some bias you have developed during your life? If you can make a guess as to what it is, tell your friend about it and watch his reaction.

4. Try to discover by questioning whether your companion has perceived something different from what you perceived in a speech. Perhaps you could question him about what the speech meant to him. Then verbalize what it meant to you and watch his reaction.

5. When you are with a member of the opposite sex, try to discover differences between the ways you and he (or she) hears something said.

6. Try to discover how poor your perception of some event is by asking other people what they heard or saw. Were the differences due to bias, sex, or simply your inability to perceive everything?

Bibliography

Barbara, Dominick A. **Your Speech Reveals Your Personality.** Springfield, Ill.: Charles C. Thomas, 1958.

Bell, R. Q. "Relations Between Behavior Manifestations in the Human Neonate," **Child Development,** 31 (1960), 463.

Belof, H. "Two Forms of Social Conformity: Acquiescence and Conventionality," **Journal of Abnormal and Social Psychology,** 56 (1958), 99.

Bernberg, Raymond E. "The Direction of Perception Technique of Attitude Measurement," **International Journal of Opinion and Attitude Research,** 5 (1951), 397.

Coffin, T. E. "Some Conditions of Suggestion and Suggestibility: A Study of Some Attitudinal and Situational Factors Influencing the Process of Suggestion," **Psychological Monographs** (1941), p. 241.

Feshback, Seymour, and Robert D. Singer. "The Effects of Fear Arousal and Suppression of Fear Upon Social Perception," **Journal of Abnormal and Social Psychology,** 55 (1957), 283.

Gilbert, H. H. "Secondary Science and Pupil Prejudice," **Journal of Educational Research,** 35 (1941), 294.

Goldhaber, G. R., and Carl H. Weaver. "Listener Comprehension of Compressed Speech When the Difficulty, Rate of Presentation, and Sex of the Listener Are Varied," **Speech Monographs,** 35 (1968), 20.

Guetzkow, H. "An Analysis of the Operation of Set in Problem-Solving Behavior," **Journal of Genetic Psychology,** 45 (1951), 219.

Janis, I. L., C. I. Hovland, et al. **Personality and Persuasibility.** New Haven: Yale University Press, 1959.

————, and F. Frick. "The Relationship Between Attitudes Toward Conclusions and Errors in Judging Logical Validity of Syllogisms," **Journal of Experimental Psychology,** 33 (1943), 73.

Jung, C. G. **The Collected Works of C. G. Jung.** Vol. 14. New York: Pantheon Books, 1963.

Kelly, Charles M. "Mental Ability and Personality Factors in Listening," **Quarterly Journal of Speech,** 49 (1963), 152.

Lewis, M., J. Kagan, and J. Kalafat. "Patterns of Fixation in the Young Infant," **Child Development,** 37 (1966), 331.

McGinnies, E. "Emotionality and Perceptual Defense," **Psychological Review,** 56 (1949), 244.

Morgan, J. J. B. "Attitudes of Students Toward the Japanese," **Journal of Social Psychology,** 21 (1945), 219.

————, and James T. Morton. "The Distortion of Syllogistic Reasoning Produced by Personal Convictions," **Journal of Social Psychology,** 20 (1944), 39.

Patel, A. S., and J. E. Gordon. "Some Personal and Situational Determinants of Yielding to Influence," **Journal of Abnormal and Social Psychology,** 61 (1960), 411.

Rogers, Carl R. "Communication: Its Blocking and Facilitation," **Northwestern University Information,** 20 (1952), 9. Also, Chap. 17 in **On Becoming a Person.** Boston: Houghton Mifflin, 1971.

Silverman, Julian. "Attentional Styles and the Study of Sex Differences" in David I. Mostofsky, ed., **Attention: Contemporary Theory and Analysis.** New York: Appleton-Century-Crofts, 1970, p. 61.

Spearritt, Donald. **Listening Comprehension—A Factorial Analysis.** Melbourne: Australian Council on Educational Research, Series No. 76, 1962.

Stromer, Walter F. "Listening and Personality," **Education,** 75 (1955), 322.

Sullivan, Harry Stack. "Tensions Interpersonal and International: A Psychiatrist's View" in Hadley Cantril, ed., **Tensions That Cause Wars.** Urbana, Ill.: University of Illinois Press, 1950, p. 79.

Taylor, R. E., and R. Eisenman. "Birth Order and Sex Differences in Complexity-Simplicity, Color-Form Preference and Personality," **Journal of Projective Techniques and Personality Assessment,** 32 (1968), 383.

Vaught, G. M. "The Relationship of Role Identification and Ego Strength to Sex Differences in the Rod-and-Frame Test," **Journal of Personality,** 33 (1965), 271.

Vernon, Magdalen D. "Perception, Attention, and Consciousness" in Paul Bakan, ed., **Attention.** New York: D. Van Nostrand Company, 1966, p. 37.

Weaver, Carl H., and W. L. Strausbaugh. **The Fundamentals of Speech Communication.** New York: American Book Company, 1964.

Wispé, Loren G., and Nicholas C. Drambarean. "Physiological Need, Word Frequency, and Visual Duration Thresholds," **Journal of Experimental Psychology,** 46 (1953), 25.

FOUR

What the listener can do to improve

If you have read carefully the first three chapters of this book, you will understand that not all this chapter will be based on research evidence. Nevertheless, there are some techniques for improving listening that have seemed to be helpful, and there are others that seem to have at least face validity. They will be described here in the belief that anyone who practices them will improve his ability to handle aurally input data.

Developing a desire to listen

Basic to the listening process is a desire to listen. It is strange that most people do not really want to listen, but to talk. Sometimes someone will ask a question but refuse to listen to the answer, breaking into the first sentence of the response with another question or an argument. Sometimes a listener will hear little of what the talker says but will spend his time planning and organizing a response. This may happen when two people are telling each other stories of their remarkable experiences while fishing or hunting. Neither seems interested in the other's story but only in relating his own. It is not difficult for anyone to remember times when he did this sort of thing.

In order to develop a desire to listen you must suppress this desire to talk. You may ask yourself sometimes whether or not it matters if you say what you are trying to get into the conversation. Obviously, if your "pseudo-listener" is not going to hear you, you are wasting your breath in the first place. It will neither inform him nor give him pleasure. Indeed, it will probably give him vastly more pleasure to have you listen to his wild tales or opinions, and by listening you will have made a firm friend. He will have found his conversation with you to be highly enjoyable.

It will help you to develop a desire to listen if you develop a desire to learn. It is often surprising to discover how much you can learn when you keep your mouth shut or when you lead a talker on with questions to develop an explanation at greater length. You may learn about the intricacies of road building, the problems of a gravedigger, the financial procedures and problems of a state government, the art and science involved in wood sculpture, and thousands of other subjects simply by asking questions of someone and listening to his answers. Knowledge of this kind will give you great pleasure—and even profit. By gathering information in this way alone, you can become a very well-informed person. In addition, you will probably be a better listener. You will probably develop a general curiosity about almost everything that will cause you to listen without trying. And it will cause you to reduce your own talking, which is usually a good thing.

If you are an adequate and well-adjusted person, you can afford to listen. People who are unsure of themselves and their judgments are often defensive. The slightest attack on one of their opinions is considered an attack on them, and they will rise, sometimes almost obsessively, to the defense. They cannot bear to be wrong or defeated. People who are well adjusted, on the other hand, are not reluctant to admit error. They do not need to be right every time, because their feelings of adequacy do not rest on one small part of their behavior. Thus the questioner who interrupts the answer may not be confident that it is safe to allow an answer. Without quite knowing it, he may think his position vulnerable. If it is vulnerable, such a person is really committing himself to an untenable position; that is, he is psychologically unable to admit any fallacies in his belief and is thus likely to be, and to remain, wrong. Even if his position is not vulnerable, he is by his impatient behavior signaling to everyone in the group that it is. A little reflection will suggest that the person who is willing to listen to the strongest criticism of his position—and let others hear it too—is confident of himself. He can afford to listen. It is said that Lincoln once remarked that if he had time to present before a judge and jury only one side of a case, he would present his opponent's side. The story is probably apocryphal, but it illustrates the point here.

You should want to listen when someone is talking to you only to achieve catharsis or to verbalize aloud to some human being something he wants to hear said. In such a case he does not want response or evaluation. He does not even want the listener to tell his own troubles. He simply wants to "get something off his chest," to think it out aloud so as to hear it himself. Until he does that, he may not understand it clearly. You can help him by listening understandingly, agreeably, carefully, and intently.

In recent years the United States, indeed the whole world, has been filled with antagonistic groups facing each other with violence and with nonviolent argument. Blacks face whites, women face men, and youths face the adult world with a bitterness and degree of contempt and discourtesy that sometimes appall anyone over thirty.

It is not easy to find someone who has tried to listen to both sides in such disputes in order to understand what both sides are saying. How difficult it is for a parent to try to find out why his son wants to wear his hair so long that "he looks like a girl," or why his daughter fights in college for the right to have men visit her in her room all night, or why both son and daughter take pride in shouting filthy words at policemen. And how difficult it is for the son and daughter to understand why their parents want them to conform to the norms of the culture in appearance and morals; to support their country and its flag; to respect the present and plan to build a better future from it; to respect themselves and their parents too.

There are reasons for all these ideological convictions, but it is not easy to get either side to listen to the other with a desire to learn. Usually listening is agreed on only to satisfy a demand by the other, and it becomes a futile exercise. No one learns anything. In such cases, listening is useful only if the listener listens because he has a real desire to learn.

Exercises

1. Ask your instructor to arrange a discussion group in your class to consider some important current problem, perhaps the problem of compelling every city and village in the country to set up an adequate sewage treat-

ment plant. Then impose one rigid rule on every member of the group: no one states a proposition or his opinion and no one presents any evidence except (1) when he is asked for it or (2) when he is using it to prepare the ground for a question he intends to ask someone to answer. Even when one member is asked a question he should keep his answers short.

If you can follow this rule, you will not be trying to get others to adopt your opinions. Instead, you will be searching for theirs.

2. Find someone whose opinions you know are usually opposite to yours. Ask him to have a cup of coffee with you and start questioning him about some opinions of his you have heard him express. Explore the depth of his knowledge, how well he can support his opinions, why he holds them, etc. For example, sometimes we hold opinions or attitudes because of some experience we had long ago and have forgotten. You will need knowledge like this to make a good judgment of the other person's motives. Be careful that your questions are not so threatening as to antagonize him.

3. If you have in your class half a dozen students whose beliefs are radical, ask your instructor to bring to the class a conservative person, perhaps a businessman, and have the radical student group question him as in exercises 1 and 2. Their questioning should seem so nonthreatening and their attitudes so permissive that the guest will not know what the students' opinions are. Afterward, the entire class should try by questioning to discover how much the group of radical students was able to learn.

4. Reverse the procedure in exercise 3, using conservative students and a radical adult from the community. It is important that the age difference be considerable, perhaps twenty or thirty years.

5. If possible, find a student in your class who strongly and rigidly believes that course examinations should be abolished. Then find another who feels just as strongly that examinations are an important part of the course. Instruct each of them privately that he is to find out what is behind the other's unwillingness to change his belief. Then let them talk.

Afterward, ask each of them to tell the class what is behind the other's belief and ask the other to respond.

6. Plan a conversational exchange in which you determine **not** to say something that at the time you really want to say. Just do not say it. Listen instead.

7. Plan a time, perhaps a dinner, when you will not make any assertions at all, even when asked a question. Make questions your only verbal responses. If someone notices anything odd about your behavior, it should tell you something about yourself.

8. Make an effort to find someone who knows something you are curious

about, perhaps some way to slow down inflation without causing un-
employment, perhaps the culture of roses. Question him, but do not make
any assertions of your own.

9. Seek out someone on the other side of the youth-versus-age conflict.
Question him at length in order to learn what his position is, how well he
can support it, how valid his statements are, where he got them, etc. This
will be a difficult exercise because you will want to engage in a dispute.
Do not do it. Just explore the talker's opinions.

Increasing your capacity to listen

Thus far we have been considering the willingness to listen. This is
an important factor in your listening behavior, but a low ability to
listen limits the listening adequacy of even the most willing listener.
It is important not only that you accept your role as a listener but also
that you improve your ability. Here are some techniques you may find
useful:

You can reflect the message to the talker. This is similar to the non-
directive technique in clinical therapy developed by Carl Rogers. The
training of thousands of clinical therapists in this technique has
proved that people can learn to do it and that it serves to keep the
talker talking. It is also a splendid technique to keep you listening. It
consists simply of paraphrasing succinctly the last statement made
to you or even making a summary statement of the whole conversation.
For instance, you might say, "You think trashing of buildings by young
radicals is not the right way for them to accomplish their objectives?"
or "It seems to me that what you are saying is that young radicals have
no respect for the present. Am I right?"

If you secure agreement to such a restatement, you must have been
listening well. But you will be surprised at how many times your friend
will say, "No! No! That is not what I meant at all." Then he will restate
his position and you should try again.

In addition to securing clarification, such a practice will sharpen
your listening so that you will mistake the talker's message as seldom
as possible. In addition, it will stall the flow of conversation on the
point concerned. The talker is likely to add evidence and examples in
order to clarify his idea, and you will probably both understand it better and learn something you did not know before. You will also understand the talker better.

The restatement—and giving the talker a chance to correct it—is similar to what someone has called the **provocative question** insofar as it stalls the conversation to allow greater development of the point at hand. There is another kind of question that moves the conversation forward from the point at hand to another thought. It is called the **follow-up question.** If you think the thought you have been asking questions about has been exhausted—that is, you have learned all you are going to learn from this person on this subject—you should use a follow-up question to get him started on a new idea.

Suppose you are trying to listen to someone talk on the subject of birth control. Early in the conversation he said that birth control has both moral and legal aspects. You have explored his thinking and knowledge about the moral aspects by the use of provocative questions until he only repeats what he has said before. A follow-up question about the legal aspects of the problem could move the discussion forward into a different part of the subject.

Restatement of the talker's message has value in addition to that of stalling the conversation on the subject until you have finished exploring his thinking. If the message is a command or an explanation of something you are being asked to do, it is important that you know what it is and how you should go about the task. A restatement by you of such instructions will tell the talker, who is perhaps your employer, whether you understand him when he says such things as "Clean up the place," or "I want these papers filed."

Exercises

1. Engage someone in conversation with the purpose of finding out everything he knows about some subject. Do not use any questions at all, only restatements. See if this will keep him talking and get him to talk about all aspects of the subject.

2. In a conversation with someone, use only restatements as your responses. Count the number of times your restatement is a fair replication of what the talker meant.

3. Repeat the process in exercise 1, but this time use provocative and follow-up questions to guide the discussion.

You must guess the talker's intent or purpose. Few messages can be understood as intended without guessing the talker's purpose. Someone once said that he liked taped laughter on television shows because without it he could often not decide whether two comedians were joking or being sarcastic toward each other. Your own response —even a question—depends on a judgment of a talker's intent. If he is joking, he may call you what would be a nasty name if he were serious. If he were serious, some damage would be done to the listening you were doing.

It is sometimes said that this inferring of motives should not be done because of the danger of error. Such a position is naive. Inferring must be done in spite of the possibility of error. Error should of course be a matter of concern, and an awareness of its possibility may reduce the number of times you are wrong and possibly make it easier for you to convert and adjust.

Such a determination of the talker's intent will also help to prevent you from being overwhelmed by a charismatic personality, an aura of competence, or high status. It will help you to identify name-calling and avoid being misled when a talker calls someone a politician and someone else a statesman. If you know his purpose, it is easier for you to identify his point of view and recognize the degree of slanting he is using. As S. I. Hayakawa once wrote, we could call a succulent, sizzling steak a first-class piece of dead cow, and what we call it would affect the listener's perception of it unless he were forewarned. Some knowledge of the talker's values and value systems will help you understand his message better.

All this really means that in order to understand a verbal message well you must understand the talker to some degree. This makes communicating with a total stranger somewhat difficult when you get above the level of asking or giving directions or talking about the weather. Even talking about the weather is easier if you know something about the other person in the conversation. Some people hate rain, for example, and others, who may have some concern about their lawns and gardens, love it.

You should be careful about stereotyping when you are making inferences about a talker. (See Chapter 3.) If you have a tendency to believe that all people in the same category are alike, you are likely to ascribe to all of them the same motives. A little reflection will tell you this is not so. Although all Quakers are pacifists, for example, many of them served in the army in the Second World War and in other wars. Some pacifists are honestly concerned about man's inhumanity to man, but it is also likely that some pacifists simply do not want to get shot at or to sleep in the mud. Some people past thirty are open minded, and some people under thirty are closed minded. You will be making many mistakes if you ascribe the same motives to all people whom you have placed in the same category. And it will cause you to listen to them badly. You will hear the wrong meanings when they talk.

In past years, much has been said about the possibility of using team teaching in large lecture sections of college classes. The advantage of this procedure is that it allows the selection of an expert in each aspect of the subject to lecture on that aspect. Thus students would presumably be getting more reliable information. In many cases, however, students have disliked this procedure because of the difficulty of learning to understand so many new lecturers. Just as they have become accustomed to one talker, he disappears and another takes over. Presumably they were bothered by the very problem you have been reading about. Before they could understand a lecturer well, they had to make some inferences about his motives, his purposes, his intent. Then they knew better what his words meant. When the lecturer was changed just about the time the listeners began to understand him, they were constantly in a difficult listening situation.

Exercises

1. When listening to somebody talk, catch yourself making a judgment about his motives. If he is a good enough friend, ask him if you were right.
2. Catch yourself stereotyping somebody, that is, inferring motives in him solely because he is a barber, a golfer, a mechanic, a banker, an officer in the army, a policeman, etc.
3. Try to discover by introspection what kinds of data you need to guess a talker's intent.
4. Do you know someone so well that you know what his motives are before he starts to talk? He probably knows yours that well too. If you do have such a friend, notice times when it is unnecessary for you to communicate with each other because each of you already knows what the other thinks. What makes this possible?
5. When someone brags, he is usually temporarily insecure about something. Try to guess what it is.

You should strive to bring the quality of your habitual listening up to the level of your optimal capacity. As with reading, we tend to listen well below our ability. This has been demonstrated in studies in which people have been tested without warning and tested with warning. There are considerable differences between the scores.

Listening at the top of your capacity, like reading at the top of your capacity, is harder work than listening without trying very much. Consequently, most people listen hard only sometimes and loaf most of the time. It is suggested here that you should learn to work harder at it. This means that you will be doing no daydreaming. You will be listening and working very hard in an effort to hear and remember what the talker says.

This is really a process of changing a habit pattern, and you should not expect to change a habit of long standing in a few days or by making a sudden resolve, like a New Year's resolution. Most of what you do when you are awake is the implementation of what someone has called reaction patterns. They govern your behavior when you need your attention on something else, and they take over almost automatically. They prevent you from changing a habit easily.

A good way to begin, however, is to change your behavior for only a few minutes at a time, when you can devote your full attention to it. This constitutes the building and learning of a new reaction pattern that, if you persevere, will take over from the old one.

Thus if you want to change a reaction pattern of relative inattentiveness to verbal messages to one of strong concentration whenever someone speaks to you, you should plan for yourself each day—ahead of time if possible—several self-assignments that you can fulfill successfully. While you are performing one of these assignments, you should give it your entire attention. Afterward, do not try to continue it. Relax until the next assignment comes up.

If you try to listen attentively all the time, you will fail. Then you will become discouraged. Furthermore, if you make your assignments too hard, you will fail and probably rationalize by telling yourself that you are just not a good listener and never will be. Always make your self-assignments easy enough that you can do them, never fail to do them, and never try to do them all day.

Before long, perhaps in a few weeks, you will discover that your new reaction pattern is becoming more and more automatic. It will take over without any effort on your part at various times of the day. When it has generalized to the point where it has replaced the old reaction pattern of semi-attention to a talker, you will have changed a poor listening habit to a good one.

In the exercises below you will find some possible self-assignments.

Exercises

1. Ask a clerk in a store about an item of merchandise. Your objective is to repeat what the clerk says word for word five minutes later. Do so. You had better have a friend listen to you.

2. Plan to concentrate your attention for five minutes at dinner on the talking done by the person sitting directly across from you. After you find this becoming an easy task, extend the time, always keeping the assignment within the realm of the possible but making it challenging too.

3. Listen intently to the first five minutes of lecturing of one of your professors. Afterward, tell a friend what he said as nearly exactly as you can. This time can be extended, too, as your ability grows.

4. Designate a chair in your fraternity, sorority, or dormitory as your "good-listening chair." Whenever you are in it, listen intently to whatever anyone says. When you find yourself tiring, move to another chair. You will find the length of time you can sit in the chair increasing as your new reaction pattern becomes more habitual.

You should try to determine whether your referents for the words of the talker are about the same as his. Reread the section in Chapter 2 on categorization. Concept referents, evoked by words, are usually subcategories with all their criterial and noncriterial attributes. It is these attributes that make an object or event meaningful.

You should realize that your referents will never be exactly the same as the talker's, because your experiences are different from his. Consequently, your listening will not produce an exact duplicate of his meanings. Your objective is to make them as similar as you can.

You can follow the restatement procedure to help your referents: repeat his message back to the speaker. You can also ask him, for instance, "What do you mean by dogmatism?" And you can tell him what meanings you have for a word, that is, what your category is like and what its attributes are.

This is one of the greatest problems of communication, and you should be constantly alert to the fact that you cannot hear exactly what a talker means to say, even if he says it well.

Exercises

1. Ask your instructor to set up a small discussion group in your class to discuss some prechosen subject. It should be a subject that will require

either some technical words or some words that will evoke strong biases. During the discussion each participant will be required to find one of these words that he thinks he does not understand in the way a talker is using it; he must then explore the talker's referent for it.

2. Make yourself ask three times each day, "What do you mean by that term?" Do not be content with a superficial answer. Continue questioning until you think you know what the talker means.

3. When someone uses a word for which you think people have widely different referents, try the technique of saying, "The meaning I have for that word is. . . . Is that about like the meaning you have?"

4. When you are listening to someone and have reason to think you are bypassing each other, ask him to specify more clearly what the referents are for some of the words he uses. Do not ask him to define them or you may merely get a dictionary definition. Ask him to describe them. For example, there are many subcategories of the category named "knife." Which one is he thinking of?

You should try to determine your purpose in every listening situation. Of course, this is not always possible. When you meet and talk with a friend, it is a little silly to decide as he opens his mouth that you are going to understand his outline and supporting material or all the details or any other specific characteristic of messages. This kind of predetermination may be done best when you attend a lecture or any other kind of formal presentation of some length. In the usual kind of conversational exchange, the purpose is at first simply to try to hear everything your friend says, even though that is not possible. As he talks, however, it is usually possible for you to decide that here the details are most important, at another time the central theme, and at another the intent of the talker.

A rereading of the list of subskills in Chapter 1 should suggest that you cannot hold all listening purposes at once and that at some time during the early stages of the talker's statement you should become aware of the one most clearly suitable for this occasion. You will, as in most cognitive activities, do this better if you do it consciously.

Exercises

1. As one of your professors begins to lecture, try to follow his outline. Write it in your notebook, including main heads and subdivisions. When you finish, you should have what looks like an outline for a speech, as indeed it is.

2. While listening to a lecture, list all the kinds of support material the professor uses. You can find a list of them in your textbook on public speaking but, in case you do not have such a textbook, here is a suitable list: story, example, illustration, comparison, contrast, quotation, fact, and explanation.

3. Listen to a speech with the purpose of locating every place where the talker slants his support material in one direction, that is, gives you evidence on only one side of the question or gives you only the evidence that will make someone or something look bad. List the evidence. Afterward, try to find some evidence in the other direction to produce a fairer picture of the person or problem.

4. Listen to a speech with the purpose of listing in your notebook every term used by the speaker that would tend to influence your attitudes. Here are some examples:
    barber or tonsorial artist
    janitor or maintenance engineer
    clerk or salesman
    died or passed away
    lie or misrepresentation

You should become aware of your own biases and attitudes. Of course, no one can be completely objective; he can be only relatively so. Everyone is biased, and everyone has a supply of words and ideas that affect him in some direction. Sometimes merely becoming aware of such trigger words and ideas, however, will dissipate their strength, often to zero. Some of them have arisen from childhood experiences. Others may be washed away simply by a realization of how unimportant they are. Still others may be reduced by a realization of the effect they have on you.

Whenever you discover such a bias it will probably help if you will (1) write it in a notebook where you can look at it from time to time; (2) talk it over with someone else, probably a friend who is willing to give you an opportunity for this kind of catharsis. If your friend, as he listens to your explanation of your bias, expresses surprise and tells you he does not feel at all the way you do, the bias may immediately lose much of its strength.

Most of your biases, if not all of them, are based on the norms of the culture. A society builds a set of requirements and taboos that are, or at least seem, important to its survival. Thus close relatives do not marry, sex deviates are segregated, family structure is preserved, people wear clothing, etc. Even small behaviors are thus prescribed: the way you cut your hair, the kind of clothing you wear under various conditions, the ways you talk to people, the kinds of games you play, the way you blow your nose, and thousands of others.

Some people chafe a little and others a great deal under these standards of behavior. As a result, the norms change, sometimes slowly and sometimes rapidly. In recent years the changes have been very fast, and some of them have concerned some of our most important norms. The norm of courtesy, for example, though still a powerful pressure in human interaction, has disappeared from the behavior of some people, at least in some situations. Also, the human body is now exposed to public view as never before. Standards of appearance and cleanliness have changed to the degree that sloppiness, raggedness, and dirtiness have in some quarters become norms in themselves.

The people who obey the new norms have developed strong biases in favor of them, enforcing them as strongly among their own subculture as the old norms were enforced when their parents were young. They have even found a kind of generalized name for the enforcer of the old norms—the Establishment.

On the other hand, the people who believe the old norms desirable and necessary have strong biases against the changing of the cultural standards. Although many of them have seen norms change during their lives, they do not seem to think those changes were important or to understand that what they are seeing now is largely a greater rapidity of change. They think the world is going to the dogs.

Of course, it may be. Some of the changes appearing on the horizon —for example, the rejection of the norm that we should be courteous to each other—would make our culture uncomfortable to live in, and it is doubtful that even the supporters of **Do It*** really want to destroy our standards of rudeness. After all, such people are courteous to each other and rude only to the enforcer of norms they do not like.

All these intellectual and emotional activities cause the development of the strong and deep attitudinal responses that we call biases. And although this short discussion has concerned only a small segment of our social standards, the principle applies to our entire behavior and value systems, even to the food we eat and the way we eat it. A member of a culture views the behavior of other members in the

---

* A book by Jerry Rubin, a radical revolutionary.

light of his own norms. He values his and despises theirs, unless they are like his. Thus he listens to someone with different norms with expectations and "knowledge" that affect the meanings he gets; the meanings he gets are often different from what the talker intends. A person with long hair dressed in worn, faded, and dirty jeans often has some difficulty communicating with a man who believes in personal neatness, especially if they meet at a "dress-up" occasion. Likewise, a girl in a mini-miniskirt who does not wear a bra is likely to have trouble talking to a woman who was reared in the 1940s.

You should realize that many of your biases toward such norms and changes in norms are based on good judgment and should not be changed. You may have strong predilections toward honesty, good faith, fairness, justice, and courtesy that you think every stable and comfortable culture should have. In short, you should have biases. You should be aware of them, however, in order that you can prevent them from causing you to get the wrong meanings when you listen or even refuse to listen.

Exercises

1. If you are a man and do not have long hair, how do you feel about long hair on a man? Do not answer this superficially. Examine your emotions carefully as you talk to several men with long hair. If you are a woman, how do you feel about long hair on a man? Your answer will probably be quite complex.

2. If you are a man who wears his hair long, how do you feel about men your age who wear their hair short, perhaps even in a butch haircut?

3. How important is the length of a man's hair? Do not answer this question with words you have heard someone else say. Examine your own biases carefully and try to verbalize them. Perhaps you should think of the culture of the entire United States, both now and through a long period of time.

4. Make a long list of recent changes in many kinds of cultural norms in this country. Try to determine which changes really matter.

5. To what degree can you "live your own life style" in a culture and ignore its norms? Does answering this question make you more fully aware of your own biases? Could it be that some of your biases are a little foolish and do not deserve shouting about?

6. Make a list of the things you feel strongly about. You are probably listing

your biases. How many of them can you defend? Can you remember when one of them interfered with your listening?

You should learn to use your spare time well as you listen. It is sometimes said that the mind can assimilate material much faster than we talk. This is probably true when the message is easy and does not require much time for cognitive structuring. It is doubtful that it is true constantly; we know that listeners do not hear all the data sent to them, primarily because it is sent faster than they can handle it. A rereading of Chapter 2 should convince you of this. But it is possible that there are times when the listener has already assimilated the information the talker is sending and the talker still stays on that subject. In such a case, the listener has some spare time.

It has been suggested that this time should be used in various ways to increase the amount of information the listener carries away with him. He can review what has been said. He can place an idea in its proper place in the structure of the presentation and judge its relation to the other parts, its relevance, value, etc. He can rehearse data that he has not yet selected for attention and thus keep it in the short-term memory system or even send it into the long-term system for later use.

What the listener should guard against, to put this in negative form, is wasting this spare time in daydreaming. If you catch yourself with a wandering mind, you should try to discover why it happened at that time on that subject. It may reveal to you some of your listening faults.

Exercises

1. As you listen to a lecture in one of your classes, find places where the professor is stalled, that is, he is still talking about some concept beyond the point where you understand it. Try to give him only enough of your attention to monitor his lecture so you will know when he goes on to a new concept. Use the rest of your attention energy to rehearse what he has already said. This will help you to remember what you rehearse. It will help to fix it in your permanent memory system.

2. As a lecturer in your class announces the third or fourth point in his lecture, rehearse the previous points.

3. Usually in a speech or lecture the talker develops each subdivision with the use of examples, facts, quotations, etc. As he uses each of these support techniques, one by one, rehearse them in connection with the subdivision he is developing. After some practice, you should reach the

point where you can almost write down his lecture after it is over, including the support techniques.

You should analyze your listening errors. Recently a man in a restaurant told the waiter, "I want a hamburger and a Hudepohl [a kind of beer]." The waiter asked, "Don't you want anything to drink?" The ensuing laughter told the waiter he had not listened well. Self-analysis might have given him some idea why and suggested an avoidance technique.

Such a procedure is called introspection, and it may not always be reliable, but it is often helpful. We cannot know, of course, why the waiter did not hear the man's order for beer, but if he should try to remember what he was thinking about at the instant the order was given it might be possible for him to find out. Perhaps he was daydreaming and should undertake the procedures of habit changing described in suggestion 3 (see Summary below) in order to improve his listening habits. Perhaps he had allowed himself to become distracted by the man's appearance or by some noise. Perhaps he had taken so much time handling the previous order that his attention was focused on that order when the man spoke. Remedies for these kinds of errors are contained in these suggestions for improving your listening. Analyzing your listening errors will tell you which remedy to use.

Exercises

1. Ask someone to give you directions to some place you know well. Then ask someone to direct you to some place you could not find by yourself. Compare what went on in your mind in the two instances. Were there any differences? What were the processes like?

2. The next time you miss completely part of what someone says to you, recall your mental process at that instant (introspect) and try to decide whether you were daydreaming, still handling information he had given you earlier, were distracted by some word that caused you to become emotional, or were in a period of microsleep (described in Chapter 2). Plan a remedy. Which of the suggestions in this chapter would seem to promise the greatest benefit?

3. Make a list of your listening errors. Can you group them into categories, that is, kinds of errors?

You should pay attention to the process of cognitive structuring as it occurs and to the time it takes. You read in Chapters 2 and 3 enough about the time required for selective attention, the search of the memory system for a fit to the stimulus pattern, the assignment of a stimulus to a category, and the perception of its meaning for you to understand that the handling of input data takes time. The time it takes is often noticeable, and you may be able to speed up the process. This is also a form of introspection. You may discover that you are really loafing at the task of finding the category or subcategory into which some item of information fits. And while you are leisurely loafing your way through this search and leisurely examining the attributes of the category to assess the meaning of the input data, the talker goes on. You miss the next item of information and perhaps several items more. You are not listening as fast or as well as you could. It will pay you to do what you can to increase your rate of handling input data.

If you discover that you are really loafing at the task of listening, it may be because you have always thought that listening is passive and that you can absorb all the data the talker sends without working. This is not so. A good listener is an active and hardworking listener. Listening probably takes as much energy as talking. We cannot loaf when we listen.

It is the same way with reading. You can take a course in reading improvement and improve your reading rate and comprehension, but if you persist in loafing at your reading—that is, reading passively— you will read no better than before.

Listening is like that too. You must work to listen well.

Exercises

1. Catch yourself in a situation where you are searching for a meaning. Perhaps you have heard a sound you do not recognize and you are thinking about it. Suddenly you have found a match for it in your memory system. How much time did it take? Could you have done it faster by concentrating more?

2. Note a time when you are searching for a solution to a problem. It may be a mechanical problem, such as how to pull a nail from a board without a nail puller, or it may be a larger problem, such as how to solve the problem of the dying cities. Note how you find one solution, examine and discard it, then search for another. How much time did you spend? Could you have speeded up the process?

3. Try to speed up your selection and search processes by determining to

speed them up. When you become fatigued, stop pressing and listen passively. What differences do you notice?

You should learn as much as you can about the process of listening. Corrective procedures planned in semi-ignorance often perpetuate error. The old statement "Practice makes perfect" should be changed to "Practice makes permanent." It is not helpful to make an imperfect technique more firmly habitual.

Much was said about this in Chapter 1. You may want to go back and read it again. In general, what was said there was that you cannot expect to improve your listening capacity or habits or willingness to listen very much in one course. The real improvement will come over a period of years.

As noted above, mere change is not necessarily improvement. The change should be guided by knowledge, and the better you understand what is going on when you listen, the more likely it is that the changes you decide to make will result in improvement.

Most people want to improve in every area of their lives that matters. Most people seem to think that listening matters. Rereading this book several times over the next few years will help you keep a knowledge and understanding of listening that would otherwise slip away. Then you may use it in guiding your listening improvement.

Summary. In this section you have read about ten suggestions for improving your listening capacity:

1. You can reflect the message to the talker.
2. You must guess the talker's intent or purpose.
3. You should strive to bring the quality of your habitual listening up to the level of your optimal capacity.
4. You should try to determine whether your referents for the words of the talker are about the same as his.
5. You should try to determine your purpose in every listening situation.
6. You should become aware of your own biases and attitudes.
7. You should learn to use your spare time well as you listen.
8. You should analyze your listening errors.
9. You should pay attention to the process of cognitive structuring as it occurs and to the time it takes.
10. You should learn as much as you can about the process of listening.

Developing your ability to evaluate what you hear

Not many of the studies described earlier in this book dealt with the evaluation of messages received. This is surprising, because when sections on listening were first written into books on the fundamentals of speech—usually public speaking books—only critical listening was discussed. For some reason, however, critical listening has not been the subject of much research. Even so, some recommendations will be made here that may improve your ability in evaluating what you hear.

You should get the whole story before evaluating it. It was Carl Rogers who once wrote that one of the greatest faults of listeners is to evaluate too early. This judgment then biases the perception of the rest of the message. From that time on, the listener hears only the data which fit the early evaluation.

An example will illustrate what is meant. A college instructor once had a student whose attitudes and behavior in class were disruptive. He was constantly interrupting others and contradicting them in an irritating way. Since the college had several guidance counselors, the instructor visited one of them, intending to ask her to counsel the student. But he never got his story told. After he had said only a few sentences, the counselor interrupted him and gave him a solution. Although he tried several times to give the counselor more information, he never succeeded. The counselor had made up her mind before hearing the whole story.

The instructor went to another guidance counselor. This counselor gave him no solution at all, but he listened carefully. Then he said he would have to talk to the student before he could make any recommendations. He talked to the student twice, at some length, before he had a solution, and he made a recommendation to the student, who changed his behavior in class and solved the problem.

What did this counselor discover by careful listening? He discovered that the student was taking a pre-law course and believed that lawyers behave in the ways he had been behaving. He was merely practicing the role he expected to play after he had received his degree in law. It took a great deal of listening for the second counselor to discover this. The first counselor would never have discovered it at all, because she could not listen.

Decisions made early affect the way we hear the remainder of the message. It is likely that had the first counselor been willing to listen to the same words the second counselor heard, she would not have received the same meanings. She would probably have heard those meanings that supported her decision and neglected the others. That is what Carl Rogers was writing about.

Exercises

1. While listening to someone explain a problem, catch yourself making a decision too soon. Then force yourself, as much as you can, to hear the rest of his story. How does it affect your decision? Could you catch yourself looking for data that supported your decision?

2. When you are explaining a problem of your own to someone else, watch him for signs of having made a judgment before you have given him all the information you think he should have. Can you warn him gently to withhold his evaluation until you have finished?

3. As you listen to a lecture or a speech, make an early evaluation. Then at the end of the lecture make another. How are they different or the same?

You should be alert to mistaken causal relations. The structure of our language is such that it is easy for a talker to imply causal relations when he does not intend to. The word "because" obviously implies causal relations; so do the words "as," "for," and "since" when used as subordinating conjunctions, but their implications are not so obvious. We do not need even these words, however, to make a causal implication, and you should be constantly asking yourself whether the cause implied is the proper cause or the whole cause of the effect under discussion.

One example may help here. In 1963, after President Kennedy was shot in Dallas, the murderer (Oswald) was seen by a woman as he shot a policeman named Tippitt. Afterward, she identified Oswald in a police line-up. When she described the identification in a television report, she said, "I knew he was the man because I couldn't take my eyes off him." This was indeed an illogical reason for knowing Oswald was the man. The two clauses do not really belong in the same sentence. Without doubt, she knew he was the man because she recognized his features, the shape of his body, his clothing, etc. It is likely that she could not take her eyes off him because she was fascinated by the experience of looking at a murderer; he was probably the first murderer she had ever seen.

This example of mistaken causal relations is not a harmful one, only stupid. You should look for other examples, and study them carefully because an understanding of this kind of error will help you to evaluate what you hear. It will probably improve your own talking too.

Of course, not all presentations of causes are merely implied by the language structure as in the examples above. Many people make their analyses of causes quite clear and overt. Then you have a chance to evaluate them more easily because you are less likely to be deceived by an implication.

Exercises

1. Examine some term paper you have written. Study all the sentences that have "because," "as," "for," or "since" beginning a dependent clause. Is the reason in the dependent clause really the cause of the effect in the main clause?

2. Find in some of your writing implications of causation that do not use the cause words in exercise 1. Do they really say what you thought you were saying?

3. Sometimes causation is presented by a speaker at a higher level than the language-structure problem in the first two exercises above. For example, he may use a type of organization like this:

    I. The problem
    II. Causes of the problem
    III. Solutions to the problem

    When you hear a speech like this, ask yourself whether the causes the speaker gives are valid and whether he has included all possible or important causes. If he has erred, does it affect his solutions?

You should ask yourself whether the speaker has done his homework well. Not all speakers analyze their subjects well so as to avoid giving their listeners anything but their best judgment, based on a thorough stock of knowledge. Most people are busy at their regular jobs, and the preparation of a major speech must be done at odd moments or at home after a full day's work. Sometimes they have subordinates prepare the speech for them, and the speaker does not know the material. Such was the case of a supervisor in Washington who described to an audience of engineers a system of buoys in the Atlantic Ocean to alert the United States to the presence of attacking enemy airplanes. He did not know his subject well and was disputed several times by engineers in the audience. At one point, he could not answer at all, and the answer was supplied by one of the listeners. His report did not engender in his listeners much confidence in what he said.

This talker was talking about his own field of competence. When a speaker is asked to speak on a subject on which he is not initially competent, he must try to become so in a fairly short time. Most do not succeed; yet they must present the appearance of competence.

It is likely that many of the speakers you hear are thus only superficially prepared. It is not difficult to notice this when you are yourself competent in the subject. You can detect naive or false statements or the misuse of terms. When you are not competent in the subject, detection is more difficult. But you should be alert to it.

You should be alert also to the danger of being egotistical in evaluating your own competence. A listener who thinks he knows the subject better than the speaker does—when he does not—may spoil the presentation for everybody.

Exercises

1. Evaluate the lectures given by one of your professors throughout the quarter or semester. Can you decide which ones had more homework behind them? If you cannot, what are the possible reasons why not?
2. Listen to any speaker. Has he done his homework well? Analyze the reasons for your answer and write them in your notebook. Explain them to a classmate and judge whether or not he believes you.

You should ask yourself whether the opinions you hear are sound. One opinion is, of course, not the same as another. An opinion of a reliable and well-informed person may have great validity if it is in the area of his competence, but when he gets outside this area, it may be worthless. Einstein, for example, had an area of great competence, but he also had strong opinions on socialized medicine that may or may not have been dependable. Opinions expressed by people of low competence and high bias are, of course, not the kind of data that should be depended on. Even conclusions based on what seems like good evidence are not necessarily "true." There may be as much evidence on which one would base an opposite conclusion. Finally, conclusions are inferences; they are not facts. It is easy to infer opposing meanings from the same set of reliable data.

Exercises

1. Your professors will often give their opinions in lectures. Usually these opinions arise from what they know about the subject, that is, evidence. If they like interruptions, ask them for the evidence. If not, ask them during a questioning period or after class.
2. When someone in your group expresses an opinion, ask him why he holds it. Do not let him give you a single answer. Pursue the subject until you have found all the evidence he can give you. If he gives you "reasons" or other opinions, pursue them.

3. Write down some of your opinions in your field of greatest competence. List beneath each opinion all the sound evidence supporting it that you can supply.

You should judge how much the speaker's biases are affecting his message. At this point it is probably unnecessary to say much more about biases and their effects on communicating. The subject will be discussed lightly again in Chapter 5, where you will be urged to control your own biases when you talk in an effort to present a fair and honest picture of whatever it is you are talking about. Here we will only remind you of the problem.

You should be constantly alert to the fact that all of us talk and listen through our bias screens. As you listen to a presentation on zoning ordinances, for example, you should wonder a little whether this talker has a personal or financial interest in what he is saying. He may be one of the promoters of a housing project, or he may be supporting it merely to help a friend who may in the future do some good for him. Not all people will do such things, of course, but so many of them will that all of us must be alert to the danger of believing messages that are designed to do good for the talker and harm to the listener. The talker in such a case does not often tell the listener of his one-sided purpose. The listener must defend himself. The old dictum "Let the buyer beware" is much more nearly universal than we like to believe.

Exercise

Attend a public hearing in your city about taxes, zoning changes, the location of a new highway, or some similar issue. Listen to the people arguing for and against the proposal and try to guess what their biases are—that is, why they are saying what they are. Are they completely honest, or do they hide their real reasons behind arguments that sound idealistic? After the meeting, talk to as many of them as you can and try to find out if your guesses about their biases were correct.

Summary. In this section you have read about these ways of evaluating what you hear:

1. You should get the whole story before evaluating it.
2. You should be alert to mistaken causal relations.
3. You should ask yourself whether the speaker has done his homework well.

4. You should ask yourself whether the opinions you hear are sound.
5. You should judge how much the speaker's biases are affecting his message.

This list could be extended, of course, by appending many items from the fields of logic and from propaganda analysis, but a discussion of each of those fields would be a book in itself.

Bibliography

Barbara, Dominick A. **Your Speech Reveals Your Personality.** Springfield, Ill.: Charles C. Thomas, 1958.

Beighley, K. C. "An Experimental Study of the Effect of Four Speech Variables on Listener Comprehension," **Speech Monographs,** 19 (1952), 249.

———. "A Summary of Experimental Studies Dealing with the Effect of Organization and Skill of Speaker on Comprehension," **Journal of Communication,** 2 (1952), 58.

———. "An Experimental Study of the Effect of Three Speech Variables on Listener Comprehension," **Speech Monographs,** 21 (1954), 248.

Cantril, Hadley, ed. **Tensions That Cause Wars.** Urbana, Ill.: University of Illinois Press, 1950.

Foulke, Emerson. "Listening Comprehension as a Function of Word Rate," **Journal of Communication,** 18 (1968), 198.

Friedman, Herbert L., and Raymond L. Johnson. "Compressed Speech: Correlates of Listening Ability," **Journal of Communication,** 18 (1968), 207.

Hackett, Herbert, Martin Andersen, Seth Fessenden, and Leslie Lee Hagan. **Understanding and Being Understood.** New York: Longmans, Green, 1957.

Hartley, Eugene L., and Ruth E. Hartley. **Fundamentals of Social Psychology.** New York: Alfred A. Knopf, 1952.

Heilman, Arthur W. "An Investigation in Measuring and Improving Listening Ability in College Freshmen," **Speech Monographs,** 18 (1951), 302.

Hsia, Hower J. "Output, Error, Equivocation, and Recalled Information in Auditory, Visual, and Audiovisual Information Processing with Constraint and Noise," **Journal of Communication,** 18 (1968), 325.

Maloney, John C. "Is Advertising Believability Really Important?" in Lee Richardson, ed., **Dimensions of Communication.** New York: Appleton-Century-Crofts, 1969.

Nichols, Ralph G., and L. A. Stevens. "If Only Someone Would Listen," **Journal of Communication,** 8 (1958), 8.

Norman, D. A. "Memory While Shadowing," **Quarterly Journal of Experimental Psychology,** 21 (1969), 85.

Orr, David B. "A Note on Thought as a Function of Reading and Listening Rates," **Perceptual and Motor Skills,** 19 (1964), 174.

———, and Herbert L. Friedman. "The Effect of Listening Aids on the Comprehension of Time-Compressed Speech," **Journal of Communication,** 17 (1967), 223.

Phifer, Gregg. "Propaganda and Critical Listening," **Journal of Communication,** 3 (1953), 38.

Pollack, Irwin. "Speed of Classification of Words Into Superordinate Categories," **Journal of Verbal Learning and Verbal Behavior,** 2 (1963), 159.

Rogers, Carl R., and Richard E. Farson. "Active Listening" in Richard C. Huseman, Cal M. Logue, and Dwight L. Freshley, eds., **Readings in Interpersonal and Organizational Communication.** Boston: Holbrook Press, 1969.

Shiffrin, R. M., and R. C. Atkinson. "Storage and Retrieval Processes in Long-Term Memory," **Psychological Review,** 76 (1969), 179.

Wiksell, Wesley. **Do They Understand You?** New York: Macmillan, 1960.

FIVE

What the talker can do to help

Like the recommendations in Chapter 4 on ways to improve your listening, some of the suggestions in this chapter have not been substantiated by research data. Some of them have been, however, and the others have a great deal of face validity; that is, experience seems to prove them true. You should try the ones that seem to fit you best and constantly evaluate them as well as you can. You can do this by checking with your listener, either by questioning him or by observing his behavior. When you find he has failed in his listening, you may decide to add to your repertoire another of these suggestions.

You should try to empathize with your listener. In general, this means you should try to hear your message as he does. This is not difficult with someone you know well. It is often true that a man and his wife who have spent their entire lives together know each other's thoughts and attitudes so well they hardly need to talk. But it is not necessary to know your listener that well. Tolstoy, in his novel **Anna Karenina,** which is said to be largely autobiographical, told this story of the way Levin declared his love for Kitty:

> "I've long wanted to ask you one thing."
> "Please ask it."

"Here," he said, and he wrote the initial letters, w, y, t, m: i, c, n, b, d, t, m, n, o, t. These letters meant, "When you told me: it could never be, did that mean never, or then?" There seemed no likelihood that she could make out this complicated sentence: But he looked at her as though his life depended on her understanding the words.

"I understand," she said, flushing.

"What is this word?" he said, pointing to the n that stood for never.

"It means never," she said, "but that's not true!"

He quickly rubbed out what he had written, gave her the chalk, and stood up. She wrote, t, i, c, n, a, d.

. . . He was suddenly radiant: he had understood. It meant, "Then I could not answer differently. . . ."

. . . She wrote the initial letters, i, y, c, f, a, f, w, h. This meant, "If you could forget and forgive what happened."

He snatched the chalk with nervous, trembling fingers, and breaking it, wrote the initial letters of the following phrase, "I have nothing to forget and forgive; I have never ceased to love you."

She glanced at him with a smile that did not waiver.

"I understand," she said in a whisper.

He sat down and wrote a long phrase. She understood it all, and without asking him, "Is this it?" took the chalk and at once answered.

For a long time he could not understand what she had written, and often looked into her eyes. He was stupefied with happiness. He could not supply the words she had meant; but in her charming eyes, beaming with happiness, he saw all he needed to know. And he wrote three letters. But he had hardly finished writing when she read them over his arm, and herself finished and wrote the answer, "Yes. . . ."

In their conversation everything had been said; it had been said that she loved him, and that she would tell her father and mother that he would come tomorrow.*

This was, of course, a remarkable demonstration of empathy, as the term is used here, and few people can ever hope to match it. But all of us approach it and with some effort we can often do much better than we do. Perhaps we fail mostly because we devote most of our attention to what we are saying and not enough to our listeners. Actually, listeners are usually sending us visual, and sometimes vocal, signals as we talk. And we are better at interpreting these signals than we know. Most of us can judge fairly well the reactions of a listener by watching him as he handles the data we send.

Empathy, however, is more than that. It is some degree of putting ourselves in the listener's shoes, of attempting to see the world and

* Leo Tolstoy, **Anna Karenina** (New York: Heritage Press, 1952), pp. 461–462.

hear the words as he is most likely to. We can use whatever we know about him and his previous reactions to help us do this. After all, we know at least a little about most of the people with whom we talk.

But what about a complete stranger, someone we have never met before? Our best guess is that he is mostly like ourselves. Human beings are far more alike than they are different. Besides, we can usually categorize a stranger by the way he looks, dresses, talks, and behaves. We pick up these signals quickly. Although you should remember that even members of the same category are different, they are more nearly alike than two people who fall into two different categories. After all, a professional bartender is not likely to see the world in exactly the same ways as a neurosurgeon. But two steelworkers are more apt to be alike than they are apt to be like two United States senators.

No doubt you have been making judgments about people and empathizing with them for a long time, thus adapting your speech so they will listen to you better; you will learn more about this process if you pay some conscious attention to it and strive to make better judgments.

Exercises

1. Try to predict the reaction of someone you know well to a statement you are about to make. Do not make this too easy by making a statement you have made to him before. Then make the statement to him and observe his reaction. If you guessed wrong, try to find out why you erred.

2. Engage in a conversation about the weather with a stranger. Make a guess beforehand about how he will react to the statement, "I hope it rains today." Then say it and see if your guess was correct. Examine your reasons for making the guess you did. If possible, talk them over with your companion.

3. It does not take very long to get acquainted and learn another person's orientations toward many things so that you may empathize better with him. Go through this process of getting acquainted with a complete stranger in one of your classes. Notice as you converse the information you get that aids you in discovering how he feels about things. Notice also the point at which you begin to relax and talk with him less guardedly. This is the point at which you begin to empathize, to know a little about how he will receive what you say.

You should prepare your listener for your message. Although there is some merit in surprise, your listener will usually hear better what you intend if his orientation at the beginning of your statement gives him a set in the right direction. If you are making a platform speech, giving him this set is one of the functions of the introduction. In a shorter interchange, doing it is more difficult but no less desirable. Doubtless you have yourself been surprised when you discovered, after having heard an entire statement of several sentences, that you had been listening with the wrong expectancy. You burst out with something like, "Oh, I thought you were talking about. . . !" You can give your listener a proper expectancy by beginning your message with a statement like this: "Let me try to verbalize my feelings about this subject. I'm not quite sure yet that I know what they are, but let me try." Or you can begin your statement with your proposition: "In my opinion, it is not possible to slow down inflation without creating some degree of economic depression. Let me say why I think that." In the latter case, the listener will then expect some reasons for your belief, probably buttressed with some kind of data. That is what he is likely to listen for.

Sometimes, as in the second example above, preparing your listener is done by stating your proposition first, if you have a proposition. A proposition is a statement of what you believe and what you intend to support, or justify. It may also be a division in a platform-speech outline or the central theme of the entire speech. Finally, it is often called the topic sentence in a paragraph of written text. You can see the topic sentences in each paragraph of George Washington's "Farewell Address." If you are engaged in a conversation with someone in which the exchanges are long enough to amount to a paragraph, you may want to say the topic sentence first. You will then follow it with reasons, evidence, explanations, etc., which your listener will then identify because they are what he will expect.

Exercises

1. Plan a statement of paragraph length with the topic sentence first. Do not tell your listener that it is your proposition and what follows is support material. Work it into a conversation and then check to see if your listener heard the message as you said it.

2. Use the paragraph message you prepared for exercise 1, but tell your listener which is the proposition and which is the support. Then check to see if he heard the message well.

3. Use the same paragraph as in exercise 1, but mix up the proposition and the support material. How did it affect the listening?

You should time your message well. This problem of timing has several aspects, and it is often quite subtle. Comedians know that their timing in presenting a joke of any kind is critical. The same witticism uttered with different timing patterns will one time create merriment and another time fall on deaf ears. You can often see this problem exposed in the performance of the great television comedians—Jack Benny, Bob Hope, George Burns—when they have a bad night. Jokes that on a good night are quite funny will not be funny at all when the timing of the punch line is too slow or too fast. Indeed, another performer once told Benny in the middle of a show that his timing was off.

Misuse of timing can cause any talker to bury important items of information in the text. You should consider the time required for a listener to handle data that are strange or difficult or data concerning some subject on which he is not well informed. In the latter case, he may have lean, seldom-used categories or none at all. Such items require more time than others. If you present such an item and follow it immediately with more items, your listener is likely to miss all succeeding items until he has finished with the first. The solution here is to give him more time. You can do this by using more support or development material on that first difficult item. You are in effect saying the same thing at greater length. You have stalled the speech in order to give your listener more time. This procedure contrasts rather sharply with another suggestion to be made about keeping the speech moving. You will need to make judgments constantly, perhaps empathically, about which of these procedures to use.

Another aspect of timing is more general. You should not present information to a listener when he is in the wrong physical or psychological condition. One junior executive once said that when he went into the boss's office with an important proposal he always planned several unimportant comments. If the boss was in an unfavorable mood, he would not present his major idea at all but merely talk about the small ones that did not matter. Later he would return and make the suggestion he deemed important—if the boss's mood had become right. Trying to talk seriously with someone whose girl has just returned his ring, who is out for a riotous night on the town, or who is exhausted from the day's work is likely to fail. Do not expect anyone to listen to you at the wrong time.

Finally, it has been demonstrated many times in many different

ways that you should say the vital parts of your message either first
or last. The middle of a message of any great length is usually the
unheard part. Whether you place the most important item first or
last depends on several factors, one of which is you; that is, you should
do it the way you do it best. If you are good at building interest as you
go through a presentation, you may want to place the most important
item last. If you are not, you should place it first because your
listeners may be bored before you say it. Other factors (the audience,
the situation, the possibility of later counterpropaganda, etc.) have
been studied thoroughly and are quite complex. If you like, you may
study them in several of the references listed in the bibliographies in
this book.

Exercises

1. Do you know someone who cannot tell a funny story so people will laugh?
   Listen carefully to his timing and see if you can catch his errors.
2. Prepare a speech in which you try to bury an item of information. You
   can do this by placing it immediately after a difficult or startling item
   that will surely engage the attention of your listeners and make them
   work hard to refute or understand it. After you have delivered the speech,
   find out how many people heard the buried item.
3. Make a plan and try asking for something important from your listener
   when he is in a good mood and when he is in a bad mood.

**If you want your listener to remember the outline of your message,
make it clear.** It is not difficult to do this. If you are telling someone
your reasons for believing something, you can number them and tick
them off on your fingers. You can review and restate them. You can
couch them in dramatic or memorable form. But do not expect him
to hear them clearly if you say them fuzzily.

It is well known that listeners can construct a good speech outline
from a rather fuzzy one—that is, do the speaker's work for him—
under some conditions. You can read about some of the studies done
to discover this by finding some of the references in this book
(Beighley,* Thompson, for instance). But the work the listener does as
he constructs an outline in his head takes some of his attention energy
and reduces the amount he has left to listen with. And when the fuzzi-

* See Bibliography for Chapter 4.

ness is quite bad, the listener becomes lost and cannot decipher the message.

Even when the listener is able to construct the talker's outline, he will probably not be able to rehearse it and thus remember it. He can do this if you (1) prepare a good outline and (2) make it clear. This means that you should give him verbal signals, perhaps rehearse the outline aloud, perhaps number the parts of the outline and, as noted above, tick them off on your fingers.

Exercises

1. Try giving a three- or four-sentence message to a friend, ticking off on your fingers several reasons why you believe something. Afterward, ask him to recite them back. If he cannot, enlist his help in finding out why.

2. After you have listened to a speech with a fuzzy outline, make what you think the speaker's outline was. Ask a friend who also heard the speech to make one too. Then compare them.

3. If you are in a public speaking class, ask your instructor to appoint two of your classmates to stand at the chalkboard behind you as you make your presentation and write your outline on the chalkboard as you talk. Did they get your outline right? If not, what could you have done better?

You should keep your message moving. Here we are thinking about a presentation of some considerable length, perhaps a platform speech. If the presentation is pitched low in terms of the sophistication and intelligence of the listeners, they will be able to handle the data rapidly and problems of timing may not exist. Instead, the listeners will have a great deal of spare time that they may use in daydreaming. One such listener to a college lecturer once told him, "I just shut my eyes and wait for you to go on." Although the talker should be careful not to bury important data in the text, he should be equally careful to keep his audience working.

This means, in part, that when you make a platform speech, you may not be able to use all the material you have prepared. While planning the speech, you must make some judgment about how much support material you will need on each idea in order for your audience to understand it. You never quite know how sophisticated an audience is until after you have spoken to them for a few minutes. Thus your guess about how much support material you will need may turn out to be wrong. You may have too much. If you insist on using all of it, you may be talking on well beyond the point where they understand you. They will become bored. You can keep your message moving by going on to the next idea as soon as you see they understand.

Exercises

1. Note in your listening experience two kinds of lecturers: one who keeps his speech moving so fast that you must be alert and work hard and one who moves his speech so slowly that you have too much time. Which do you like better? Which one teaches you most?

2. There are many ways to make a speech boring, and not all of them are the fault of the speaker. Notice a speech or lecture that was boring because the speaker talked about ideas long after you had understood them. List the support materials he used during these boring periods. How much time did he spend on them?

3. Make some guesses, or inferences, about the reasons speakers sometimes do not keep their speeches moving.

You should stimulate your listeners. As Kapp once wrote, "A person is receptive when he is stimulated, loses receptivity when he is bored." New and worthwhile ideas, the kind that make the listener say, "I never thought of that before" or "I wish I had said that," are usually stimulating. Discussion of problems of some immediate importance to the listener may be stimulating too. The presentation of a new aspect of an old problem will usually awaken interest. In general, unless your message stimulates the listener to thoughts that seem worthwhile to him, he will become bored.

This problem is not simple, of course. Some people have very narrow interests, and some are more egocentric than others. Degrees of sophistication and intelligence vary widely. Stimulating a listener who is intelligent and knows a great deal about many different things requires greater sophistication from the talker, but such people have wide interests, and the selection of the subject need not be so carefully considered. You may be confident, however, that they will not be stimulated by trivia.

Exercises

1. Do you know someone whose ideas seem to stimulate your own thinking and develop your interest? Analyze his talking and try to discover how he does it. Try to find out if he stimulates others too and, if so, what kind of people they are.

2. Observe the conversations that you have with others. What proportion of your own comments attracts the attention of others and becomes the subject of the conversation. Are they worthwhile comments, or are they trivia?

3. Analyze conversations you hear. Make a list of the ideas that seem to stimulate people. What are they like? What do they tell you about the people who are stimulated by them?

You should be specific enough. It is more difficult to categorize general statements than statements that are more specific. This is probably less true of listeners who are accustomed to dealing in generalizations, but it is usually necessary for a listener to find an application or a specific example under the generality in order to find a category that provides a good match for it so as to perceive its meaning. Providing specific examples for the listener makes the cognitive search easier and faster. In addition, it provides greater likelihood that the listener will think of the same subcategory you are considering. Thus bypassing may be reduced or avoided.

You will understand the differences between general and specific statements if you look at a speech outline you have made and imagine using only the subdivision sentences in your speech and none of the support material. If you have a long outline, you may make such a speech as long as you like. You will use no support material, no examples, illustrations, evidence, quotations, etc. Unfortunately, many beginning speakers make speeches like this, and so do many experienced but poor speakers. Such a speech is quite difficult for a listener to handle unless he already knows most of it.

Exercises

1. Observe your cognitive behavior when you listen to a talker who speaks only high-level generalizations. Can you understand his general statements—or even some of them—without finding a specific example subsumed under them? If some and not others, try to find out what the difference is.

2. Prepare a speech by the process described in the paragraphs above: make a long outline with many first-level subdivisions. Do not use any support material. Present it to your class and ask them to criticize it. Do not tell them in advance what you are about to do or what your purpose is.

You should be clear. You have already read about making your outline clear if you are making a platform speech, and about providing specific examples to clarify generalities. Another important but not well understood aspect of clarity lies in your word choice and sentence structure.

Of course, you can never say exactly what you mean. You can only approximate it, and you can say what you think you are saying. Unfortunately, many talkers say something quite different from what they think they are saying. Consider these examples of obfuscation and try to discover just how the talker went wrong:

> If I've learned anything in this course it is that I cannot make straight lines. So I'm going to have to ask you to apologize if my lines are crooked.
>
> I find myself to be a pledge to a fraternity that will be rooming with an active next week.
>
> This thesis then is designed to explore the two issues involved, the Federal Communications Commission versus the Community Antenna Television interests.
>
> Read the following statements by inserting them in the blank space in the sentence below.
>
> Please, without any talking in the appropriate blanks, give your name, sex, date, your date of birth, and the class section.
>
> Just before class my title page was run over by a motorcycle while I was standing on a corner.
>
> However, evidence from this statistic was not confident enough to say there was a significant difference in the connotative meaning of speech between any of the groups.
>
> Speech will be interpreted as both theoretical and oral communication.
>
> Sixty-five percent of our members have voted unanimously to reject the board's offer.
>
> How many people do you employ, broken down by sex?
>
> The completed questionnaire was collected in the meeting room before the person left.
>
> The Leamington Hotel is the first stop for the limousine for the airport and costs only $1.50.
>
> At least he has produced no evidence of the validity of his claims and hence is a mere assertion without foundation of fact.
>
> Well, I am not going to answer that question directly, but I will say this: I believe there is still, we have got great savings, I believe that we have got to offer things in a better packaged way, we've got to do better advertising and above all things let the public buy when they think they are getting a bargain and not worrying about what is going to be the possible future of some possible future action.

The demand for employment security has been intensified, exceeding seniority to guaranteed employment.

In the above quotations, the talkers probably knew quite well what they intended to say. They just did not say what they thought they were saying.

Clarity depends on other factors too, one of which is presenting enough information and another excluding irrelevant and obfuscating information. A teacher in a school of nursing had trouble making clear to her students the process of administering an injection. She told them something like this: "First you pull the plunger of the hypodermic syringe out to the mark indicating the number of cc's you want to inject. Then you turn the bottle of vaccine—or whatever—upside down and push the needle through the rubber membrane at the top of the bottle into the fluid. Then you push the plunger in and pull it out again to the right cc mark and, finally, pull it from the bottle." Her students did not invert the bottle and they did not pull the plunger of the syringe out before pushing the needle through the rubber membrane. The reason was that the teacher did not give them enough information. There was no understanding of the reasons for these procedures and some of the students did not even hear them. After the teacher explained that the reason for pulling the plunger out before inserting the needle into the bottle and pushing it back in after insertion was to create a pressure in the bottle so as to avoid drawing air bubbles into the syringe, and that the reason for inverting the bottle was to make sure the needle was immersed in fluid, her students got the message. She had not given them enough information to make her message clear.

Finally, the purpose of an adjective or adverb is to signal to the listener which subcategory you want him to attend. If you want to talk about "big red dogs," do not merely say "dogs." Your listener may be attending his category of little white dogs or even coyotes.

Achieving clarity is a constant and ongoing problem with most talkers. Several popular magazines, for example the **New Yorker,** collect published statements that are often hilarious because the talker or writer said something he did not intend to say at all.

Exercises

1. When you get back from a professor a term paper you have turned in, look for marks he has made on it. When you find one indicating that you did

not write what you thought you were writing, save it. Make a collection of them.

2. Add to your collection of misstatements things you say and hear others say that are obviously not what you or they thought was being said.

3. If you are in a public speaking class and your professor assigns a process speech (a type of speech in which you explain a process in temporal order), collect examples of a speaker failing to make the process clear because he omits some information, perhaps a step in the process.

You should take advantage of preliminary tuning whenever you can. This principle is closely related to preparing your listener for your message. It differs, however, in the sense that preliminary tuning is a process of raising the level of vigilance to a point where the listener will be alert to almost anything, whereas creating an expectancy develops an alertness in a predetermined direction.

Eisenson, Auer, and Erwin attribute the first use of this term to Young. It was a carefully developed process in the speaking of Mussolini, Hitler, Huey Long, and many modern revivalist preachers. For them it consisted of creating an atmosphere that suited the purpose of the speaker by the creation of crushing crowds, blaring or soft music, ritual and panoply, massive choirs, and many other devices.

Most of these extra rhetorical devices are beyond the reach of most talkers, but some things may be done anyway. If you are about to make a platform speech, you should not prevent the chairman from knowing about your accomplishments and status. Sometimes a kind of false modesty causes a speaker to conceal information that would cause his listeners to attend more carefully if they knew more about him.

Sometimes you can choose the time when you present a message, and you should choose the time when some preceding event or discussion has built just the right mood for it. For example, a solution to a problem being sought by a committee will be rejected if presented too early; but if, after everyone has had his say, a good solution is given the committee members, they may listen carefully. The process of listening to and rejecting suggested solutions sometimes puts committee members in the right frame of mind to listen to a good one. Besides, the hour may be getting late and people may be tired and in the mood to listen. This is not a kind of manipulation but a technique for getting a hearing. Presumably, if there are faults in the solution, it will be rejected like any other poor plan. But it will have been heard.

Even events extending over days and weeks may develop such preliminary tuning in listeners. Prolonged overwork or hunger, extended public or private problems, consistently good or bad news, etc., can tune an audience to the point where they will listen more carefully than they would have done before. It is said that Winston Churchill in 1940 and 1941 would never have played the heroic role he did had he appeared on the scene earlier. Indeed, he did appear earlier in the 1930s with warnings against Hitler and was not heard. In 1945, after his audience changed again, he was quickly turned out of office. Obviously, there is a time to send your message and a time to hold it. When listeners are tuned properly, you will be heard.

Exercises

1. When you attend large gatherings of people to hear a speaker, notice their degree of preliminary tuning. Are they excited? Expectant? Vigilant? Alert? Try to figure out why.
2. Watch a Billy Graham crusade on television. Note as many things as you can that seem designed to get the audience in the proper mood, or tuned. Then read some journal articles about the ways Graham organizes his crusades. (Perhaps you should do the reading first.)
3. Speech journals have articles about the ways Dwight L. Moody, Mussolini, and Hitler tuned their audiences. Read them and prepare a report for your class.
4. Attend a lecture on campus. Make a list of things that would have served to accomplish a preliminary tuning of the audience.

You should reduce the number and kinds of inferences your listener must make. It is known that the making of valid inferences from spoken data requires some high degree of intelligence. Unless you verbalize your proposition, about half of an average audience will miss it. Of course, there are some good reasons for leaving your proposition implicit, but they concern the acceptance of it, not the hearing of it. If you want your listeners to know where you stand, you had better tell them.

This problem was discussed in Chapter 1 under the heading of "Kinds of Data" in connection with explicit and implicit data. Your listeners have a chance to hear what you say explicitly, but they must generate their own inferences about the meanings you only imply. They have many inferences to make about you, about your intent, about the referents you have for the symbols you use, etc. And not everyone makes the right inferences. Many times when we make an inference, we do not realize it is an inference. You may be accused, if you do not make your meanings explicit, of saying things you did not say.

Exercises

1. Try to catch yourself making inferences while someone else is talking to you. Why did you make them? That is, what in the talker's behavior implied the meanings you got from his message?
2. Catch yourself implying some meaning. Why did you do it? Were you afraid of offending your listener. Were you lazy?
3. Much meaning is communicated by implication. Listen for examples of this kind of communication and try to judge whether the meanings could better have been explicitly verbalized.
4. After you have said something to a friend, ask him what you said. Analyze his answer. How much of it was inferential?

You should do what you can to prevent premature evaluation. Much of the time the causes of this serious listening fault are beyond the control of the talker. Psychotics, high dogmatics, people with short tempers, etc., may evaluate prematurely no matter what the talker asks of them or how he goes about his task. Most people are not like that, however, and are willing to give the talker a chance to have his say.

Perhaps one way to help you get your story heard before it is judged is simply an honest and straightforward request for fair play. Most people are essentially fair and able to hear the other side of an argument through. It is said that when Wendell Phillips spoke in England during our Civil War he used this technique to get a hearing. He was a Northerner, and he was facing a hostile audience of cotton-mill workers who were out of work because the Northern blockade of our Southern coastline prevented American cotton from reaching their mills. Thus they were heavily involved. Phillips proposed that they hear him out and that if, after having heard him, they still disagreed, then he could only say that they had given him a fair deal. It is not known whether their premature evaluations were temporarily suspended or not, but it is known that they listened to him and were impressed.

You may help to prevent the development of premature evaluations by starting softly and thoughtfully. Do not shock your listeners by making extreme and dogmatic statements before you have presented your evidence. Indeed, one of the uses of inverted organization, where the proposition is presented last, is to prevent this kind of shock. If your audience is prepared for or even convinced of your proposition before you utter it, there may be no shock at all. Sometimes, of course, you may never make your proposition explicitly, allowing your listeners to form it for themselves, but this involves the danger described in the preceding section.

Finally, without their knowing that they are being taught, you can teach your listeners by your own behavior how to consider both sides of a quarrel, how to reserve judgment, and how to judge with moderation. This is one of the self-controls all listeners surrender in some degree to the talker the moment they begin to listen. Their behavior is to some extent controlled by him, and his by them.

Exercises

1. Find someone who tends to respond angrily when one of his ideas is attacked. See if you can attack one of them and still get a thoughtful, considerate hearing from him.

2. Try to teach someone implicitly by your own behavior to reserve judgment on one of your statements until he has heard you out. You must do this by demonstrating that kind of behavior yourself as you listen to him.

When you are trying to explain or describe some object or event, you should tell your listener what it is not as well as what it is. For a good many years educators have been telling teachers they should never use negative instances because learners might err and consider them to be positive, that is, correct. For example, a teacher of nurses once said she would never use a true-false test in one of her classes because her students might learn the false statement. Recent research has demonstrated, however, that in concept learning the inclusion of negative instances improves the understanding of the concept and quickens its acquisition. Inspection of some of the references for Chapter 2 will confirm this (for example, Hull, Looney and Haygood, Sutherland and McIntosh, Wason).

Exercise

Prepare a definition of something that is difficult to explain or understand. Do not look it up in the dictionary. You are about to describe a category, perhaps to list the criterial and noncriterial attributes. Include several examples of objects or events that would fall into the category and explain why. Then name several that would not be included and explain why they would not; that is, show that they do not have the criterial attributes of the category.

You should be aware of your own biases. You have read a discussion of listener's biases in Chapter 4. You may want to go back and read it again. The only difference between the listener's biases and those of the talker lies in their respective positions. Since the talker has control of the conversation, at least temporarily, he has some advantages and may be able to control the direction of the conversation. Insofar as he can retain control, he can to some degree determine what information is sent.

The talker has a serious obligation not to send untruths and half-truths. Of course, there will always be dishonest and devious people, so this obligation will probably never be universally fulfilled. Even among honest people, however, the obligation is not always met. We tell it as we see it. It is not often that anyone can tell it as it is, because he cannot see it as it is.

Nevertheless, a fair-minded talker can do much to present an objective picture. It is quite possible for two people to view the same facts and agree on them but still arrive at opposing positions in the end, because their values are different. Different values can cause them to weigh the facts differently.

As a talker you should, when suitable, present both sides of a question. And you should present the side you do not believe as fairly as the side you espouse. If there is a third side, you should present it too.

You should also be alert to the dangers of name-calling. It really does matter what you call something or someone, because the listener will probably place him in the category you have named. For example, the category named by the word "politician" is usually different from the one named by "statesman." You can unfairly influence your listener by your choice of words.

You can also talk dishonestly by the process called slanting, discussed in Chapter 4. For example, you may influence your listener's attitudes by describing a man with all the negative details you can think of, using no positive details at all. You may unfairly influence attitudes toward the welfare program by describing it with details either for or against. A good example of this kind of reporting is Stuart Chase's book **Government in Business.** In this book, Chase described all the governmental failures in business that he could find.

You can sometimes talk dishonestly by failing to tell your listener what your objectives are. For example, two residents of a township in a Midwestern state toured the township, stopping house by house to convince the voters that a low-cost housing project would be a bad thing for the township. Actually, their bias was personal; they had expensive homes across the road from the planned project, and they feared loss in real estate values. The housing project was later built in a different part of the township and turned out to be an asset to the community. These two men misrepresented their motives. If you have something to gain from the acceptance of your message, honesty demands that you tell your listener. It will help him to evaluate it fairly, which is his right and duty.

Finally, no one likes a manipulator. Everyone likes to make up his own mind, and a manipulator tries to prevent that. When we discover we are being deceived and manipulated by someone, we usually react —perhaps overreact—negatively. We will, in the words of Emerson, ". . . shrink from him as far as he has shrunk from . . ." us.

Exercises

1. Can you remember when you discovered that someone was using you to help accomplish some objective that would help him and not you? How did you feel about it?
2. Attend a public hearing on some question of great local concern. Make a list of the name-calling terms you hear. Then find for each one another name that evokes a different kind of meaning.
3. Listen to someone describe some public program such as welfare, aid to the blind, or federal support for research. List the advantages and disadvantages he presents. Was he slanting? If so, how did he do it? Do you think he meant to?

You can attract and re-attract the listener's attention when it ebbs. As you read in Chapter 3, the fluctuating of attention is not under the control of the listener. No matter how determined he is to listen and concentrate, his attention will ebb into the periods Haider calls microsleep. You can, however, help him break the pattern.

We are talking here about relatively long messages, such as the platform speech. For short one-sentence interactions, the ebbing of attention may not be a serious problem, but when a listener sits for a long period trying to listen to one person talking, it can be a serious problem. If, as a talker, you are concerned about it, you should use some techniques to re-attract your listener's attention as it recedes.

Essentially, the techniques you use should contain the elements of variety and novelty. Of course, variety means novelty. Every change in the signal means that it is a new signal. Such changes may be accomplished by moving about on the platform, thus sending the vocal signal from a different direction; raising or lowering the pitch or loudness of the voice; changing the vocal inflection and timing patterns; and changing the subject—that is, keeping the speech moving.

Mere loudness does not help, but a **change** in loudness does. Thus, making the voice quieter re-attracts the listener's attention by breaking into the cycle just as well as making the voice louder does. It provides a different signal. In the same fashion, changes in all the voice variables will change the signal.

You can devise other ways to change the signal too. You can be active on the platform. No one ever fell asleep when Billy Sunday preached, partly because he was so active. Sometimes he broke chairs into kindling wood in the pulpit. Sometimes he stripped off his coat, necktie, and shirt. Sometimes he slid across the floor, imitating a runner sliding into third base. His voice was constantly changing too, sometimes rising to a shout.

When you are presenting a message of some length, you should remember that if your listeners are to pay attention it is you who are responsible for it.

Exercises

1. As you listen to a speaker or lecturer you find it easy to attend, try to discover what the speaker is doing to help you.

2. When you listen to a dull speaker, make a list of the things you think he should do to attract and re-attract your attention.

3. If you are in a public speaking class, watch your listeners closely in order to note when their attention is ebbing. Then do something, such as turning to the chalkboard and picking up a piece of chalk. Does it help?

Summary. You have been reading in this chapter about these fourteen ways that you can, when you talk, help your listener:

1. You should try to empathize with your listener.
2. You should prepare your listener for your message.
3. You should time your message well.
4. If you want your listener to remember the outline of your message, make it clear.
5. You should keep your message moving.
6. You should stimulate your listeners.
7. You should be specific enough.
8. You should be clear.
9. You should take advantage of preliminary tuning whenever you can.
10. You should reduce the number and kinds of inferences your listener must make.
11. You should do what you can to prevent premature evaluation.
12. When you are trying to explain or describe some object or event, you should tell your listener what it is **not** as well as what it is.
13. You should be aware of your own biases.
14. You can attract and re-attract the listener's attention when it ebbs.

Bibliography

Eisenson, Jon. **The Psychology of Speech.** New York: Appleton-Century-Crofts, 1938.

——, J. Jeffrey Auer, and John V. Irwin. **The Psychology of Communication.** New York: Appleton-Century-Crofts, 1963.

Kapp, Reginald O. **The Presentation of Technical Information.** London: Constable, 1948.

Nichols, Ralph G., and L. A. Stevens. **Are You Listening?** New York: McGraw-Hill, 1957.

Thompson, Ernest. "Some Effects of Message Structure on Listeners' Comprehension," **Speech Monographs,** 34 (1967), 51.

Tolstoy, Leo. **Anna Karenina.** New York: Heritage Press, 1952.

Whyte, William H., Jr. **Is Anybody Listening?** New York: Simon and Schuster, 1952.

Wiksell, Wesley. **Do They Understand You?** New York: Macmillan, 1960.

Appendixes

The material in these appendixes is an expanded and more technical presentation of parts of Chapters 1 and 2. In the process of expansion, a great deal of material has been added on the subjects of the teaching and testing of listening capacity that seemed not to be important to the main purpose of the book but that may be of help to the student who wants to pursue these subjects further.

The short appendix on compressed speech has been added because of its relation to processes presented in Chapter 2.

References cited in these appendixes can be found at the end of Appendix B. It seemed more useful to the reader to group them thus, since in many cases a single reference is useful for more than one of the areas concerned.

The teaching and testing of listening

Whether or not people can be taught to listen better depends on many factors. The foremost problem is concerned with the question of what is the process we call listening. It will be the purpose of this appendix to explore this question first in terms of how people have attempted to teach listening and second in terms of their testing. The testing is necessary, of course, in order to find out whether anything has been learned and, if so, what.

Listening: a separate behavior

It is sometimes said that listening and reading are the same process. It is also sometimes believed that listening is perfectly correlated with intelligence; that is, any intelligent person is a good listener because he has a good memory. Large vocabulary, good reasoning ability, and oral memory span are also sometimes said to be synonymous with listening ability. Before discussing the teaching and testing of listening, it will be useful to consider the evidence that listening is a separate human activity like reading.

Newman and Horowitz studied listening in a novel way that will be discussed in the testing part of this appendix. Their discoveries are of some interest here, however. First, they found that listeners distort more than readers do but produce fewer omissions. Their listeners had higher scores on "style"; that is, they could reproduce sentences more nearly exactly and with better structure than readers could. Finally, asking a listener to write what he heard or a reader to tell what he read always produced lower scores. This was probably the most interesting of their findings. Apparently, asking subjects to change the mode of expression from the mode of input caused some loss of data. This would suggest that the cognitive structuring of input data is not the same for listening and reading. This conclusion was supported by a finding that although readers and listeners received about the same amount of data from the same message, they missed—that is, did not perceive—different items. The conclusion was supported also by the fact that the correlations between scores on listening tests and scores on silent reading tests are usually only in the .50s. The correlation coefficient is an indication of how much two factors vary together—that is, how much, when one goes up, the other goes up too. If they are quite closely related in this way, we begin to believe they are, or stem from, the same process or that one is causal to the other. A correlation of .50, however, suggests that only 25 percent of the variation between them is caused by their relation to each other or to factors common to both. The other 75 percent is then believed to be caused by other factors. They are more unlike each other than they are similar. Thus in this case a great deal of the variation between these two kinds of scores is unaccounted for, suggesting that reading and listening are not the same thing.

Caffrey isolated a factor he called "auding" (meaning listening) by using nine tests, although the reading factor was strongly related to it. Caffrey and Smith found somewhat stronger indications of the auding factor in a later study. Hanley also found some evidence in tests of verbal facility, voice memory, auditory synthesis, and some others, that listening to verbal messages is not the same as reading. Spearritt used thirty-seven different kinds of tests and clearly isolated a listening factor that did not belong to the others he found. It is Spearritt's study that will be described here because it will lead us into the problem of what we teach when we teach listening.

Although Spearritt tested several hypotheses, his main hypothesis was that the variance among scores on listening comprehension tests can be accounted for by tests in reasoning, verbal comprehension, attention, and memory, and no separate factor of listening need be postulated. Many of the tests he used were standardized tests prepared by the Educational Testing Service, the Australian Council for Education Research, and others. Eight tests of listening comprehension were prepared and standardized by Spearritt and included in the test battery. One of these contained material from STEP (Sequential Tests for Educational Progress) prepared by the Educational Testing Service. These listening tests were named as follows by Spearritt:

1. Listening vocabulary
2. Listening for general significance
3. Listening to note details
4. Listening for inferences
5. Listening to a short talk
6. Listening to spontaneous talk
7. Listening to boys' talk
8. Listening to girls' talk

The other twenty-eight tests were grouped under such general headings as inductive reasoning, deductive reasoning, general reasoning, verbal comprehension, attention, auditory resistance, meaningful memory, rote memory, and span memory. Some tests were administered orally and some were taken in printed form, for example, arithmetic and Thurstone's reading test.

Presumably, if the skills and capacities required to do well on Spearritt's listening tests could be accounted for by the skills required to do well in reasoning, verbal comprehension, attention, and memory, a factor analysis would load the correlations in those areas and no separate factor for listening would appear. Listening could then be considered an amalgam of those four capacities and we could improve it by teaching them.

Such was not the case. The data on the listening tests did not fall into the loadings on other factors. Spearritt found these seven factors in his data:

1. Inductive reasoning
2. Deductive reasoning
3. Memory span
4. Memory (both rote and meaningful, but somewhat different between boys and girls)
5. Auditory resistance
6. Verbal comprehension
7. Listening comprehension

It is interesting to note, in view of the discussion of sex differences in Chapter 3, that the memory factor showed sex differences. In addition, Spearritt found some indication of a separate factor of listening comprehension for girls.

No further work on this problem has been reported in the literature since Spearritt made his report. Unfortunately, Spearritt's work is not well known, probably because it was published in Australia. This evidence seems to show that listening is a kind of human behavior in itself, separate from reading, from memory, and from other intellectual behaviors, although dependent on them as they are probably dependent on it.

The teaching of listening

Before describing the ways that have been used to teach listening, it would be helpful to understand that any appraisal of the results of teaching are dependent on the kinds and quality of the test used to measure those results. Unfortunately, many of the tests used were not as good as Spearritt's, and judgments on teaching methods should be reserved until an understanding of testing methods is developed. Furthermore, in many studies the tests used were not designed to measure what was taught.

The effectiveness of teaching. It is probably safe to say that about half of the programs used in teaching listening have apparently been successful. Hollow gave daily twenty-minute lessons to 5th graders for six weeks and found significant improvement. Pratt taught 6th-grade students only five lessons at weekly intervals. Lewis trained high school students for seven months. Irvin, Nichols (1948), Brown (1954), Johnson and Richardson, and many others have found significant improvement during listening training. On the other hand, many have not. Petrie found no improvement, nor did Voelker, Meyer, Hollingsworth, Orr and Friedman, and many others.

Courses in listening. Typical of some teachers of listening is the report by Niles, who had students list the factors they believed affected listening and compare them with Nichols's list, read a speech about listening, make inventories of their own listening habits, determine their own purposes in listening, observe the good and bad qualities of speakers, restate the position of an opponent in an argument, and do role playing in parlor games. Some of these seem to have rather high face validity, but others are at least mildly questionable.

Typical of some other courses is a program of teaching described by Renwick. Renwick prepared a course plan, which was taught by high school teachers, designed to teach listeners to receive data better and to listen critically. The receptive skill was taught by providing practice in recognizing stated or implied main ideas, distinguishing details, relating details to the concepts they supported, and discounting irrelevancies. The critical listening was taught by providing practice in evaluating argument and persuasion. There was a great deal of discussion in the classes after the listening was over and some introspection and self-evaluation. Although the Michigan State listening test was used as a pretest and posttest, it was not used to evaluate the program. Instead, students did their own self-evaluation. The program itself was evaluated by asking the students, after discussion in small groups, to report their evaluations of it. In general, they approved the course but sought material easier to outline and to understand. Renwick decided he had designed a good course.

Finally, K. Johnson found that at the end of his teaching experiment his experimental group had improved significantly but his control group had not. Eleven weeks later, however, he found that the experimental group had regressed to its original level before the training program, and the control group, "to the great embarrassment of the department," had regressed even further, falling back far behind their original level. Johnson blamed the regression on the balmy Minnesota spring weather, but the effect seems more likely to have been the result of the confusion now existing about what constitutes the listening process and the relation between the teaching and the tests used.

What do we teach when we teach students to listen better? Hollingsworth (1964) used ten Listening Skill Builders from the Science Research Associates program and ten tapes selected randomly from the Educational Development Laboratory's **Listen and Read.** Each of these lessons was fifteen minutes long and the program ran once a week for twelve weeks.

Neither of these teaching techniques, used in separate experimental groups, generated any more improvement than the control group demonstrated. In another study Hollingsworth (1966) taught twenty-nine middle-management personnel in a large industrial concern as follows: each two-hour class period had a Listening Skill Builder, a lecture-discussion period, an experience in note taking, a written exercise, and an assignment for reading in a textbook (**Are You Listening?**). The lecture titles included "Why Study Listening?" "Listen Well," "Bad Listening Habits," "Listening and Note Taking," and "Selective Listening." Hollingsworth used the Brown-Carlsen Listening Comprehension Test for his pretest and posttest and found that scores went up 50 percent. But he used no control group. In his other study he had found that both the experimental and control groups improved significantly but about the same. He would have had significant improvement in that study if he had not had a control group.

It will be illuminating to describe a number of teaching programs that have been reported in the journals. Dow published a report of the way listening was taught at Michigan State. The researchers' objectives were to increase knowledge and understanding, improve skills and abilities, and develop better attitudes toward and appreciation of listening. In order to accomplish these objectives, they taught students something about the importance of listening, how to take notes, and how to locate the main points in a message. They presented exercises in listening to informative material and seven-to-twenty-minute lectures after which the listeners were tested. Listeners scored their own answers. Critical listening was taught in about the same way: teaching, practice, testing.

Erickson taught 130 college students for about four hours scattered over a twelve-week period. The first session was a lecture on the importance of listening, the need for a purpose in listening, getting the main idea and supporting details, listening for specific information, and the purpose of the experiment. Then came fifteen exercises from the McCall-Crabbs **Test Lessons in Reading** and three from Brown's book **Efficient Reading.**

Students were asked by Irvin (1954) to construct a code of listening manners, to make lists of their own listening weaknesses and strengths, to list the distractions in the room, to write down central ideas in an oral message, to engage in what he called "round-robin listening activities," to stand and repeat what the instructor had just said, to repeat a set of oral instructions given them, to practice outlining oral speeches, to select one main point and the supporting data from a speech and write them down, to introspect and report points where their minds began to wander, to take notes only on the introduction and conclusion of a speech (after which they were asked to write an outline of the body of the speech), and to list words, phrases, and illustrations that caused them to react emotionally.

Six training lessons were used by Heilman in which he pointed out a number of listening habits that "authorities believed differentiated between good and poor listeners," built a respect for listening, explained projection, showed the students how their own ideas colored their reactions to speakers and what they said, and provided practice in recognizing main ideas.

Johnson and Richardson taught listening in three ways to college students. The first group heard six ten-minute taped lectures, one per week. The first lecture dealt with listening. The other five treated subject areas within the field of speech. Students were tested after each lecture. The second group listened to four classroom student speakers, each of whom had prepared in advance short-answer test items that were administered immediately after the four speeches were finished. Thus students had to listen to all four speeches as if they were going to be tested on all of them, since they did not know in advance which one would be the subject of the test. The scored answer sheets were given to the speaker to let him see how well he had communicated and then to the listeners to let them see how well they had listened. The third group was a public speaking class. Students here had to listen, or sit and pretend to listen, to about a hundred speeches. They were not tested on the speeches, but the Brown-Carlsen Listening Comprehension Test was used for the pretest and posttest. The first two groups improved significantly, but the third did not. Improvement in the first two groups was almost exactly the same. One wonders whether the improvement was due to improved listening or to improved sending of the message by the speaker.

Orr and Friedman tested a hypothesis that listeners might be able to handle aurally input data at higher speeds if they were given a precis of the message. It did not help. Abrams and others have discovered that taking notes or having an outline in hand before the message is presented does not help.

Many others have taught listening classes and described them in the journals, but the ones reported above are a fair sampling. Teachers of listening have tended to do just about what has been described here.

Commercial training programs

Recently a number of commercial firms have prepared training programs designed to improve listening skills at various levels. The Educational Development Laboratories, for example, have prepared training tapes that combine listening and reading for grades one through college. Most of the programs contain fifteen tapes and seek to develop these skills among others: recognizing sounds in the environment, finding the stated main ideas in a story, noticing the correct order of happenings, listening for details, noting likenesses and differences between people and countries, recognizing causes and effects, learning how to recognize clues to predict outcomes, using the five senses while listening in order to share experiences described in poetry, making mental pictures of something that is being described, understanding how attitudes and customs are affected by the setting, learning to recognize the climax in a story, identifying the elements of exaggeration that make a tall tale amusing, learning to recognize such propaganda techniques as name-calling, testimony, and bandwagon, learning to distinguish between fact and opinion, learning to reason, etc. The list above is specified for the 3rd and 6th grades, and it is not complete. The teaching of listening is integrated with the teaching of reading and thinking. Tapes are provided and studying may be done individually or in groups.

Ella Erway has developed a listening training program for the McGraw-Hill Book Company. It was designed for use in public speaking classes at the upper high school and college levels. There are seven progressive programs, all recorded on audio tape, that can be used individually or in groups. The subskills developed are as follows: to state the central idea, to list the main divisions of a speech, to identify support material, to identify emotional appeals, and to evaluate the speaker's language. Obviously, most of the messages presented to listeners are speeches, ranging up to eight minutes in length.

The Listening Skills Program developed by Science Research Associates was designed for the first six grades. In the lower grades, the Listening Skill Builders concern awareness of pitch and volume and the language for describing them, following directions, developing sentence patterns, the concept that sound implies action, awareness of fantasy, and the use of content to develop vocabulary. In grades 4 through 6 the Skill Builders include training in such skills as auditory discrimination, instant recall, following directions, remembering sequences, listening for main ideas and details, listening for cause and effect, visualizing and listening for mood, making inferences, and distinguishing fact from opinion. The lessons are recorded on tapes or discs and may be used individually or in groups. Pretests and posttests are provided, but no data are available on them.

The Dunn and Bradstreet course prepared by Nichols and called the Complete Course in Listening is recorded on cassette tapes. The first tape is a lecture by Nichols, and the last is a pretest and posttest. The other four tapes contain practice skills: overcoming distractions, detecting central ideas, maintaining emotional control, and evaluating the message. The course may be completed in eight hours or extended to thirty by the addition of reading in several books. No data are provided on the tests.

Conclusions

Enough description of teaching techniques has been presented here to demonstrate the uncertainty about what should be taught. Much more could be said. The keystone to this arch of confusion was added by Baker when he wrote, "I believe I am teaching important aspects of listening whenever I teach spelling, punctuation, matters of style, speech criticism, or oral reading."

The teaching of listening is at present somewhat like the "curing" of stuttering. It has been said that in some cases anything will stop a stutterer from blocking and in others the best clinical therapy in the world will have no effect. One stutterer was "cured," for example, when his father angrily dumped a basketful of fish over his head; others are cured simply by maturation, that is, by no therapy at all. Still others have been cured by moving (where drinking water was different!) and by excising a portion of the tongue.

And so it seems with the teaching of listening. Petrie has raised a serious question about whether listening is a unitary skill or a combination of skills, and if it is a combination of skills, what are they? Bakan listed five precarious assumptions that workers in this field seem to make:

1. That listening is a unitary skill.
2. That uniform training should be given to all subjects.
3. That listening is teachable.

4. That listening is independent of other psychological variables.
5. That the effectiveness of listening training can be evaluated at the end of the training period.

Thus it seems no more certain that listening is teachable than it does that stuttering is curable. Nor does it seem tenable, in spite of what Bakan wrote, that listening is a composite of peripheral skills. The great variety of skills selected for teaching and called by the generic name "listening" suggests that if listening is an aggregate of skills, each skill must be almost specific to the occasion. When K. Johnson set out to plan his program, he "considered the situation in which the college student was engaged and determined that a course in listening designed to help the student in the classroom lecture-type situation would constitute the most beneficial approach." To Johnson, then, the skills involved in this kind of situation, as he perceived them, became **listening** skills and his program a **listening training program.** It is quite doubtful whether a different person facing the same problem and trying to imagine the skills involved would have made the same list Johnson made. It is quite certain that most other researchers have constructed their lists with other situations in mind. Thus hardly any list is at all like another, and all listening training programs are different.

We have been concentrating on what Gray and Wise have called external factors:

> That attempts to evaluate and improve these external factors may be entirely worthwhile nobody can deny, provided they are made with due regard for recognized scientific method; no suggestion is intended that the end product of listening—comprehension and retention—might not be improved by increasing the efficiency of these external factors. But careful studies in listening . . . need, among other things, further research in the analysis of listening as a "discrete linguistic function"; they need, moreover, further research than subjective guesses on the influences which affect the process, be they intrinsic or extrinsic.

Perhaps, as Gray and Wise suggest, listening is a unitary skill. Perhaps beneath all these external factors or peripheral skills lies a cognitive skill that generates some degree of proficiency in all of them. Some suggestion of this may be found in the discussion in Chapter 2 of the basic rate of cognitive processing of additional data. Orr and

Friedman, in the study cited above, hypothesized that one limitation on a listener's ability to handle speeded speech is his inability to process the data as fast as it is sent. Their study was an attempt to reduce the burden of the listener by limiting the number of choices he had to make.

Finally, it seems obvious that there is a tendency among teachers of listening to settle on a group of peripheral skills and call them listening. When those skills are learned, they assume the student has become a good listener.

The testing of listening capacity

It should be clear that when listeners are presented a message to listen to and know they are going to be tested, it is not their **listening habits** that are being tested but something else. Usually we say their **listening capacity** is being tested, that is, their optimum listening ability. Of course, it is possible that something different is being tested, for example, the degree to which they are motivated. It has been demonstrated that the interestingness of the message listened to has no effect on listeners' test scores (Spearritt) when the listeners know they are to be tested. Presumably, knowledge of the upcoming test motivates them because they want to score well on the test. If, then, having been warned of a test and perhaps told some reason why the test will affect them, interestingness affects the scores, it might be said that the listeners were not motivated in spite of the warning. The test would then be a measure of their motivation and not of their capacity.

Even so, an experimenter does his best to motivate his listeners and usually must assume that he is successful. On this assumption he bases his right to call his listening test a test of **listening capacity.** But he makes no claims to be measuring **listening habits.**

Something was said in the section on the teaching of listening about the tendency of a teacher or experimenter to decide rather arbitrarily what skills listening consists of. Then he calls his lessons a listening training program. The same problem exists in testing, but it is even more complex and confused. Sometimes such a teacher does not even test what he has been teaching. It seems almost as if he believes listening to be a complex of subskills and that improvement in some of these subskills will carry over into all of the others. Consequently, the teacher seems to reason, any good "listening" test will measure the results of his efforts.

Testing what is taught

Erickson used this training program: he lectured on the importance of listening, the need for a purpose in listening, getting the main idea and supporting details, listening for specific information, and the purpose of the experiment. Then he presented eighteen training exercises, fifteen from the McCall-Crabbs Test Lessons in Reading and three from Brown's **Efficient Reading.** His pretest and posttest, however, were the Brown-Carlsen Listening Comprehension Test, which was constructed to measure the ability to listen for details, follow oral directions, recognize transitions, understand word meanings, and find the main idea in a lecture. There are a few items that also test the ability to make valid inferences. Apparently, Erickson did not test what he had taught.

Meyer and Williams taught listening to 10th graders. Their training program included such activities as these: students read, discussed, and wrote about listening, were encouraged to improve their listening, were tested on the morning's announcements to determine their listening habits, and wrote essays on listening improvement. They had sixteen such practice listening exercises, along with some messages read by the experimenter and some played from tape recorders, on which they were tested. The pretest and posttest used were the Brown-Carlsen. Some, if not most, of the time during the sixteen training periods was spent on things other than those tested at the end of the course.

Many studies have done this in varying degrees and with varying degrees of success (Hollingsworth, 1964, 1966; Johnson and Richardson, Voelker, McDonald, for instance). Petrie used a combined procedure. He **taught** verbal organizational ability—that is, the ability of the listener to perceive the organization of a spoken message. He **tested** this ability with the Goyer Organization Test and with a test of organization that he prepared himself. But he also used the Brown-Carlsen Listening Comprehension Test, only a little of which measures what he taught. He found significant gains on the Goyer Test and on his own test. Strangely enough, like about fifty percent of the studies in listening improvement, he also found significant gains on the Brown-Carlsen test. It is not easy to explain this. Perhaps there **is** some transfer from one listening subskill to another. More likely, the work Petrie did in teaching skill in perceiving the organization of a speech included, at least incidentally, some training in enough of the skills measured by the Brown-Carlsen to generate improvement. Perhaps also the listeners learned enough about the test format of the Brown-Carlsen that they could do better on the second administration of it without any real improvement in the listening subskills measured.

Many experimenters have made their own listening tests or used tests already made for other purposes. Many of these tests seem to have fit the training program only indifferently well. Kibler, Barker, and Cegala used thirty-four items that Kibler had developed in his thesis. They were "validated against the speech content," but no one knows what subskills they measured. It seemed a matter of little concern. There is little doubt that it was a good test of something because of the conditions under which it was made. It is likely that it was a test of the listener's ability to retain content, probably at varying levels of detail.

What listening tests measure. K. Johnson used parts of the reading-comprehension section of the American Council on Education's Co-operative English Test for his test. Giffen and Hannah used the STEP listening test. Heilman made a test that measured the abilities of getting the main idea, hearing the facts, and making inferences from the data heard. Blewett, for one of the early studies in the measurement of listening capacity, made an eighty-item test in which forty items concerned names of people, places, streets, buildings, and distances, directions, colors, and fabrics, and forty items measured the ability to draw conclusions from a series of related ideas, to make inferences, and to identify speaker attitudes. Dickens and Williams used a cloze procedure test that consisted of eliminating words systematically and asking listeners to supply them. Cloze procedure seems to tap many variables apparently not taught by Meyer and Williams, for example, knowledge of the deep structure of the language and the predictability of form-class and function words, arising partly from the structure of the language and partly from semantic implications. Goldhaber and Weaver used test items that measured knowledge of details such as dates, names of people and institutions, inventions, and events.

M. Johnson reviewed all the peripheral skills used by these and other experimenters and selected eleven of them for her test, designed for grades 4, 5, and 6. Here is the plan for her test:

Listening Subskill	Number of Items
Following oral directions	4
Recognizing transitions	1
Making inferences	3
Differentiating among contextual clues	1
Getting the main idea	3
Listening for sequences of ideas and data	2
Getting the details	7
Listening for meaning in imagery	2
Perceiving causal relations	3
Perceiving noncausal relations	4
Getting the critical elements	5

The test was standardized in rural and urban schools and gave evidence of adequate internal consistency (.77) and validity. Validity was suggested in part by the average difficulty indexes for the three grades 4, 5, and 6: .43, .50, and .57, respectively. If listening is an aggregate of subskills, this test promises to become a satisfactory measuring instrument.

Rossiter developed a listening test for college students that may become useful for adults and perhaps for high school students. He developed eleven messages about one and one-half minutes long. Each message was read by a different person, including both men and women. Listeners responded to six test items after each message, two of which measured ability to hear details, two the ability to hear general ideas, and two the ability to make valid inferences from the data presented in the messages. As expected, the inference items were the most difficult. The ability to hear details and to hear general ideas were almost exactly equal. The test was standardized on university students and the reliability was .76. Rossiter's belief that the three subskills measured by the three types of items were independent though related was supported by the fact that items of each type, when considered a separate subtest, correlated more highly with the total test score and with their own total subset scores than with the other subtests. The test contains sixty-six items, twenty-two on each of the three subtexts, and takes about forty minutes to administer.

Perhaps the most original test was the one devised by Newman and Horowitz, the results of which were presented at the beginning of this appendix. Some of their subjects read and some heard from tape a little story. Half the readers and half the listeners were then asked to write the story verbatim. The other halves of each group were asked to tell the story back verbatim into a tape recorder. The reproductions of the story were then typed and marked off by vertical slash marks into what Newman and Horowitz called "bits," which Sincoff later called "isolates," of meaning capacity. These isolates were considered to be the smallest meaningful units of language and to be equal in the amount of meaning they evoked. Thus the experimenters were able to count the number of isolates correctly reproduced and determine the proportion of the data sent that the listeners received. This is probably the closest anyone has come to computing this proportion, but the validity of the procedure is still in doubt.

James I. Brown (1951, 1955) selected subskills on the basis of pronouncements of the Commission of the English Curriculum of the National Council of Teachers of English, conclusions reached by Nichols (1948) in his study of factors in listening comprehension, his own study of diagnostic tests in silent reading, and the opinion of eleven experts, mostly chosen from among the members of the Vertical Committee on Listening of the National Council of Teachers of English. Items were prepared for subtests to measure these skills and tried out in two experimental forms. The final form of the test was administered to 8000 high school students and 300 college freshmen. This is the structure of the test:

Part A: Immediate recall (This requires keeping a sequence of details in mind until a question is asked that requires thinking back over the sequence.)

Part B: Following oral directions

Part C: Recognizing transitions

Part D: Recognizing word meanings

Part E: Lecture comprehension (This assesses the ability to listen for details, get the central idea, draw inferences, understand the organization, and note the degree of relevancy of one part of the lecture to the others.)

Although Brown found the correlations among these five parts of his test to be low enough that he decided they were tapping different subskills, Bateman, Frandsen, and Dedmon contended that his breakdown of Part E was not correct. They did a factor analysis of responses to the items on this part of the test and found only two factors, both of which were impure and unstable. In fact, the factors were so impure that the experimenters could not tell what they were and hesitated to name them. Finally, they called one listening for details (eleven items) and the other making inferences (seven items). Three items were not loaded on either factor, nor did they cluster together. The Brown-Carlsen is the most widely used copyrighted test and probably has been since 1955.

The Educational Testing Service has constructed (1955) even more carefully than the Brown-Carlsen, if that is possible, a series of four listening tests adapted to student abilities from the 4th grade through the second year in college. They were designed to measure these sub-skills:

1. Plain-sense comprehension
   a. Finding the central theme
   b. Remembering significant details
   c. Remembering simple sequences of ideas
   d. Understanding denotative meanings of important words
2. Interpretation
   a. Understanding implications of main ideas
   b. Understanding implications of significant details
   c. Understanding interrelationships among ideas and the organizational pattern of spoken material well enough to predict what will be likely to come up next
   d. Understanding connotative meanings of words, inferring meanings from context, and understanding how words may be used to create a mood or aesthetic feeling
3. Evaluation and application
   a. Judging validity and adequacy of main ideas and distinguishing fact from fancy and proved statements from opinion and judgment
   b. Judging the extent to which supporting details accomplish their purpose, distinguishing relevant details from the irrelevant, and judging whether or not additional information is needed to prove the speaker's point
   c. Criticizing organization and development of spoken material, being aware of self-contradictions by the speaker, and recognizing the devices the speaker uses to influence the listener's thinking
   d. Judging whether the speaker has created the intended mood or effect and, if he has failed, why
   e. Recognizing what the speaker wants the listener to do and the

ways in which the speaker's ideas may properly be applied in new situations

Thirty-five percent of the test is devoted to part 1, 40 percent to part 2, and 25 percent to part 3. Since the test is only thirty-five minutes long and two forms contain only seventy-two items and two others eighty items, some of the complex skills, especially in part 3, are tested only by a few items. Inspection of the list above, parts of which are omitted here, will show that some of the skills are really two or three skills, and it could be said that this test assesses the ability of the listener in twenty-eight skill areas. Eighty items seem to spread thin over such an array.

This list was prepared by more than forty college, high school, and elementary teachers. The test was written and evaluated by these teachers, with the help of the technical staff at ETS. It has come into wide use in research and in school programs.

The importance of good testing. It will be worthwhile before concluding this section on testing to say something about the process of constructing a reliable and valid test. Too many times a test is whipped together in the mistaken belief that anyone can make a good test simply by writing questions that demand answers. Such a test maker has no idea whether his test has construct validity. He does not consider the question of reliability, nor does he know that some of his items may have negative item-test correlation coefficients. He does not know the scatter of difficulty indexes of his items nor that the nature of this problem may produce scores that lead him to believe his subjects are an atypical sample. Many of the reports described in this section—and others not described here—have used unanalyzed tests that may have been so unreliable and invalid that they may not have tested their hypotheses at all. In truth, no one knows what they have tested nor how well. We read their conclusions, couched in proper statistical language, ". . . the null hypothesis was rejected (p.=.001, 160 d.f.)," and accept them as truth. They may have no truth in them at all. Unfortunately, many scholars who know a great deal about their subject matter and about statistics know little or nothing about measurement. Not many have analyzed their tests as did M. Johnson, Rossiter, Spearritt, Brown, and the Educational Testing Service. This suggests that we must take with several grains of salt statements by teachers and testers of listening that they have been able to teach or test successfully.

The use of compressed speech in research and teaching

This book cannot be concluded without a short exposition of the use of compressed speech in the study of listening and in the teaching of substantive material. Compressing speech may be done in several ways. In general, it consists in shortening the time a message requires, thus increasing the number of words said per minute and the rate at which data are sent to the listener. Increasing this rate increases the burden on the cognitive operations of the organism, and the increase is limited by the capacity of those operations to handle data.

When Rossiter was developing his listening test, he presented his fourteen messages on audio tape at three speeds: 175, 233, and 265 words per minute. He found that the mean scores for the seventy-four listeners at each rate declined from 44.33 at 175 wpm to 34.95 at 233 wpm and to 29.63 at 265 wpm. This phenomenon is partially explained in Chapter 2. It will be worthwhile to explain it further here, even at the risk of some degree of repetition.

It is generally accepted that the capacity of the human organism to handle data is limited. For example, Broadbent found that "two perceptions plus two switches of attention" required one and one-half seconds. Moray found the perception of single digits to be faster: it took only a quarter of a second for his subjects to make an echoic (repeat-back) response, but this was quite a different task from the one posed by Broadbent. Moray also found that his subjects could handle not more than four digits per second. Kristofferson measured what he called "minimum dwell time" (a period of time during which the organism remains in a state before switching) and found that the minimum dwell time plus switching time demanded 130 milliseconds. Broadbent called this combination of minimum dwell time and switching time "perception time." Although the time durations reported in the literature are not in exact agreement, there is agreement that they provide a ceiling on the organism's capacity and that the system is almost constantly overloaded, resulting in loss of input data.

The researchers named above, and scores of others, dealt with auditory input. Sperling found similar results with visual input. In general, the organism must centralize its attention on data input through one channel, although there is disagreement about the ability to monitor other channels (Moray and Barnett). A good deal of research has suggested that a subject can attend one channel adequately while sampling at least one other channel, probably periodically. Moray and Barnett presented four stimuli (letters of the alphabet) within two seconds over each of four channels. Subjects performed less well than when two channels were used; when two channels were used, subjects could report all the stimuli from one channel correctly and then recall some data from the other channel in a disorganized way. Obviously, the organism was overloaded and, equally obviously, subjects were able to monitor the unattended channel at some low level while performing adequately the assigned task on the selected channel when the task was not too difficult. Moray (1960) found that errors in performance increased as the presentation rate increased, suggesting that at some point the rate of data input exceeded the capacity of the organism to handle the data even when only one channel was used and the selection was made in advance.

Most researchers in this area posit two memory systems, short-term and long-term (Norman, 1969; Broadbent, Deutsch and Deutsch, Trabasso and Bower, Morton). Shiffrin and Atkinson suggest three: the sensory register, wherein (at least in the visual modality) memory decays in milliseconds; the short-term storage (STS), wherein memory decays in less than thirty seconds unless rehearsal takes place; and the long-term store (LTS) where Shiffrin and Atkinson assume memory to be permanent. The subject must search this LTS with input data for a match in order to categorize the data and thus assign meaning to it. To search all the LTS would be prohibitive, so most researchers, including Shiffrin and Atkinson, posit some kind of "content-address-able" or "self-addressable" system that generates a smaller ensemble, or set, which is then searched. The search process is usually consid-ered a recursive loop in which locations or "images" are selected for examination. The response-generation process then makes a decision that results in a continuation or termination of the search, the send-ing of inhibitory impulses to some part of the reticular formation, or the selection of the incoming data for conscious attention. These processes are often delayed by intervening items, proactive interfer-ence, irrelevant data, intrusions, overloading, etc. Sutherland and McIntosh have developed a theory that they call "the conservation of attention law," which fits the experimental data reported here and elsewhere. Their law posits a limit on the **amount** of attention the sub-ject has to use. The more he attends to and learns about cue A, the less he will learn about cue B. This has been called "attention energy" by Weaver and Strausbaugh.

There is some scant evidence that the processes involved in data input and retrieval can be speeded up with practice. Part of it has been reported in the literature on improvement of reading rate and comprehension. Leckart, Keeling, and Bakan, Leckart, and Bakan and Leckart found that "looking time" decreased with practice.

Presumably, if the rate of cognitive structuring of aurally input data could be raised, a listener could hear more. This is not to say that he would; he might instead use the time thus gained for daydreaming. But just as we hope that increasing one's ability to read fast will re-sult in faster reading, so we must hope that a listener whose rate of cognitive structuring of data has been increased will use his extra time in handling more data. Perhaps this rate can be raised by some kind of practice, just as it is raised in programs of reading improve-ment. This process **might** be the basic skill underlying all the so-called peripheral skills that have been discussed in this book. It seems useful here to describe some of the research already done in the use of compressed speech and its application to the listening process.

Research in rapid speech began with the use of a reader saying words rapidly, the speeding up of a recorder or record player, and the cut-and-splice method on auditory tape. For some years, compression of orally spoken text has been done electronically by one of several methods. The discussion here will be limited to research done in these ways under the general subject areas of the optimum rate, some general effects of compression, techniques for the use of the time saved by compression, listening efficiency, and programs in use now or in the immediate past to use compressed speech in the teaching of subject matter.

The optimum rate

Fairbanks, Guttman, and Miron in 1957 did a model study in which they prepared two texts of 1554 and 1573 words on meteorology. They described the texts as "expositions of factual information, descriptions of instruments, definitions of concepts, and explanations of procedures." Recorded at 141 wpm, the tapes were compressed 30, 50, 60, and 70 percent. Trainees at Chanute Air Force Base scored about the same at 50 percent compression (282 wpm) as at zero compression on carefully analyzed achievement tests. Above that level (60 percent compression), scores fell off rapidly.

Shriner and Sprague presented short commands to 3rd-grade children and found that they had shorter reaction times at 50 percent compression than at 30 percent or 70 percent, but performance fell off rapidly above 50 percent.

Wood found that children in Montgomery County, Maryland, could "cope successfully with single-sentence commands compressed to 400 wpm," but performance was better below 250 wpm. Foulke compressed taped speech at 25 wpm intervals up to 400 wpm and found that above 250 wpm performance fell off significantly.

Gore presented spoken text to blind high school students at normal rates and at 33⅓ percent compression and found no difference in comprehension. McCracken compressed eight passages from the Diagnostic Reading Tests to 50 percent and found no differences in comprehension between this rate and the normal rate for either men or women at Wayne State University. Goldhaber and Weaver found that for college freshmen comprehension fell off somewhere between 175 and 325 wpm.

Reid found that at 325 wpm college students learned as much as at 175 wpm, and that at 275 wpm achievement scores were better than at the normal rate. This is one of only two studies to report this effect.

Other studies found achievement falling off slightly but not linearly as rate was increased.

Orr (1968), who has done a great deal of work in this area, concluded that while results of all these studies differ somewhat, the range of 275–300 wpm seems to be the optimum rate if maximum comprehension is the goal, and the rate chosen may depend on several factors such as intelligence of the listener, complexity of the text, and difficulty and strangeness of the subject.

Gerber was the most optimistic in a report in the **Journal of Communication:** "The most obvious general conclusion within the terms of this study is that time-compressed speech is highly intelligible. . . . One may conclude that speed of speech can be effectively doubled without impairing intelligibility." One should note, however, that Gerber was writing about intelligibility, not comprehension. If the equipment is good enough, satisfactory intelligibility may be obtained at higher rates than satisfactory comprehension. Unless the compression is adequate, however, comprehension may be limited by low intelligibility or the two factors combined.

Some general effects

The studies cited above, and others, have reported some interesting effects in addition to the results of achievement testing. Sticht reported that listening is as effective as reading for low- and medium-aptitude subjects and that intelligence affects comprehension as rate is increased. Goldhaber and Weaver reported that comprehension was greater for college freshmen when the difficulty, as measured by the Flesch Readability Formula, was at their own level. Barabasz found retention after one week to be equal when the speech was compressed and when it was presented at the normal rate. But Woodcock and Clark found a sleeper effect similar to that found in some of the Yale studies. Achievement scores after one week rose for subjects who heard compressed speech but not for subjects who heard the same speech at the normal rate. Many of the studies reported here found variability among subjects to comprehend compressed speech, especially at very high rates. At least part of this variability was attributed to variance in intelligence, but unknown factors seemed to account for some of it.

Friedman, Orr, and Graae, in their final report to the U.S. Office of

Education, summarized the side effects of their study of compressed speech as follows:

> Listening to the practice materials for approximately an hour without interruption presents no difficulty. . . . A rest period of three minutes after each ten minutes of exposure is no better and is possibly more detrimental to the achievement of good comprehension than an un-interrupted flow. The use of incremental increase in rate over this period from about one-third faster than normal to two and one-half is not any better or worse than presenting all material at two and one-half from the beginning.

Use of time saved

Not much research has been done to develop ways to use the time saved by the compression of speech to add to the learning by the student. Fairbanks, Guttman, and Miron used the two long tests de-scribed above to test double presentation of the compressed message. Only 50 percent compression (282 wpm) was used. Subjects learned slightly more by hearing the compressed version twice than other subjects did by hearing the normal version once, but not significantly more. Their data were presented thus:

	50% Compression		0% Compression	
	Single	Double	Single	Double
Scores in percentage correct	58.0	65.4	63.8	67.6

Thus there was no significant difference between the two double presentations, but one used twice as much time as the other.

Woodcock and Clark also tested the effectiveness of the double presentation of compressed speech but in both immediate and split conditions. In the immediate condition subjects heard the tape twice in the same listening session and were then tested (the same tech-nique as was used by Fairbanks et al.). In the split condition, the sec-ond presentation was delayed one week. They found that the delay did not help.

Loper used Fairbanks's original messages and presented them on videotape with visuals and by sound tape recorder. He found that adding visuals to the verbal messages did not increase comprehension scores at either normal or compressed speeds.

Finally, Fairbanks et al., using their two long messages, added redundant sentences (variant repetition) to the text to bring them up to their original time length after compression. Of sixty items on the achievement test, the text on thirty was thus expanded. The text on the other thirty items was left as in the original. Both the semantic and technical aspects of the expansion were very carefully done. Testing showed that subjects marked significantly more of the expanded items correctly but at the expense of the unexpanded items. Thus the total scores did not change.

It may be seen that the techniques for using the time saved by compressing oral speech have not been widely studied, and the published studies have produced equivocal results.

Efficiency of listening to compressed speech

Fairbanks and his collaborators were impressed by the greater efficiency of listening to compressed speech embodied in the data shown above from their study of repetition. Since the compressed versions of their messages used only half as much time as the uncompressed versions, obviously subjects were learning much more per unit of time when they listened to rapid speech.

Woodcock and Clark computed the listening efficiency of their subjects by this formula:

$$\text{Listening efficiency index} = \frac{\text{Treatment mean} - \text{Test-only mean}}{\text{Listening time in minutes}}$$

Treatment mean was the mean score of the experimental group, and Test-only mean was the mean score of the control group. The subtraction of one from the other was presumed to account for prior knowledge. They found that elementary school children listened most efficiently to speech at some rate between 228 and 328 wpm. Sticht computed the efficiency index for his low-, medium-, and high-ability groups and found that efficiency increased sharply as rate was increased to 275 wpm and did not fall off significantly even at 425 wpm.

It is generally recognized in the literature that although efficiency is an important factor in the educational process, its importance is diminished as actual learner achievement falls toward the tolerable limit set by the situation.

Teaching with compressed speech

Although it may be said that any experiment in which compressed speech is presented to subjects who are then tested on the content of the message is teaching, attention here will be restricted to those reports or notices of educational programs of some duration. The following programs are examples of perhaps fifteen ongoing or recently finished teaching projects.

In the fall of 1967, social studies for 4th-grade pupils and history for 11th graders were used for teaching in the Ohio State School of the Blind in Columbus, Ohio. Compression started at 10 percent and increased in 10-percent increments until comprehension fell off. No report of this program has been published.

The Teaching/Learning Resources Center of the Centennial Schools of Warminster, Pennsylvania, installed a program in 1967 to improve listening skills, reading, and modern-language instruction. A program using compressed and expanded speech to develop listening skills for gifted, average, and slow learners was begun in Alameda County, California, in January 1968. The program encompassed 1000 students, 40 teachers, and 30 schools.

The Library of Congress prepared tapes for the Spartanburg County School for Handicapped Children in South Carolina. These tapes contained expanded speech for mentally retarded blind children. In a similar fashion the Library of Congress is providing tapes, records, and machines for many blind or retarded individuals and for institutions serving the blind and retarded.

No program at the college or high school level designed to teach a course or a subject such as history by using compressed speech has been reported, or at least found, although some universities are contemplating the installation of dial-access systems that will allow a student to listen to a compressed lecture from his dormitory. Friedman, Orr, and Graae have studied the learning of lecture material with college students using novels and historical, psychological, and geological material. At rates no higher than 300 wpm, they have found college students able to learn as well as at normal rates of presentation.

The blind, of course, have long been experimenting with and experiencing speeded speech. The most common method is simply increasing the speed of a variable speed recorder or record player, even though the pitch rises linearly as the speed is increased. The Library of Congress and the American Institute for the Blind supply recorded materials (even entire magazines, issue by issue) in low-pitched male voices to make the increases in pitch more easily tolerable. In addition, many millions of dollars have been spent to provide equipment for blind people.

Foulke (1966) mailed tapes of texts to blind people, compressed at 180, 225, 275, 300, and 350 wpm. He asked them which rate they preferred to listen to. Presumably they considered both comprehension and efficiency. They preferred these rates:

25 percent preferred 225 wpm
45 percent preferred 275 wpm
23 percent preferred 300 wpm

Perhaps the attitude of blind people can best be seen in this letter written by a blind man to the Center for Rate Controlled Recordings at the University of Louisville, although it is probably not safe to believe that sighted listeners would react in the same way:

Dear Editor:

In the Newsletter which arrived today, there is a comment to the effect that no use has yet been made of compressed speech as a study technique. While this is technically true, I should point out that a good many of those of us who are blind have been using speeded-up playback for a good long time for our reading purposes.

For the past 15 years, as a college student, and now as a college teacher, I have been playing back all my records at speeds up to 60% faster than the recorded speed. Granted this distorts the voice, but it is not intolerable if the original recording is clear and is done with a man's voice with reasonably low pitch. I know of other blind students who quite consistently play their tapes back at double speed, since on tape recorders there is no middle ground.

. . . Many of us are hopeful that materials will be available in compressed form, but it is obviously going to be a long time before most of us will get material in compressed form. In the meantime, a big help for many of us would be an inexpensive tape recorder with variable speed control. . . . I assure you, many of us have long been speeding up recorded materials and would not remain sane very long if we had to go back to dragging along at 160 wpm. But if you can bring us to compressed speech also, more power to you.

Sincerely yours,

It was suggested earlier that cognitive structuring of input data might be the process underlying all listening. If so, training in this process might improve performance in all the subskills we have thus far been teaching and testing.

References

Abrams, Arnold. "The Relation of Listening and Reading Comprehension to Skill in Message Structuralization," **Journal of Communication,** 16 (1966), 116.

Bakan, Paul. "Some Reflections on Listening Behavior," **Journal of Communication,** 6 (1956), 108.

———, and B. T. Leckart. "Complexity Judgments of Photographs and Looking Time," **Perceptual and Motor Skills,** 21 (1965), 16.

Baker, William D. "Listening—A Functional Part of Composition," **Journal of Communication,** 6 (1956), 174.

Barabasz, Arreed F. "A Study of Recall and Retention of Accelerated Lecture Presentation," **Journal of Communication,** 18 (1968), 283–287.

Bateman, David, Kenneth Frandsen, and Donald Dedmon. "Dimensions of 'Lecture Comprehension': A Factor Analysis of Listening Test Items," **Journal of Communication,** 14 (1964), 183.

Blewett, Thomas T. "An Experiment in the Measurement of Listening at the College Level," **Journal of Communication,** 1 (1951), 50.

Broadbent, D. E. **Perception and Communication.** London: Pergamon Press, 1958.

Brown, Charles T. "Studies in Listening Comprehension," **Speech Monographs,** 26 (1959), 288.

Brown, James I. "The Objective Measurement of Listening Ability," **Journal of Communication,** 1 (1951), 44.

157

——. "How Teachable Is Listening?" **Educational Research Bulletin,** 33 (1954), 85.

——. "The Construction of a Diagonistic Test of Listening Comprehension," **Journal of Experimental Education,** 18 (1955), 139.

Brown-Carlsen Listening Comprehension Test. New York: Harcourt Brace Jovanovich, 1955.

Caffrey, J. "Auding Ability at the Secondary Level," **Education,** 75 (1955), 303.

——, and T. W. Smith. "Preliminary Identification of Some Factors in the Davis-Eells Games." Cited in Donald Spearritt, **Listening Comprehension—A Factor Analysis.** Sydney: Australian Council on Educational Research, 1962.

Campbell, Ronald F. Q. "Teaching Oral Communication in College: Approaches and Innovations," pamphlet, Department of Communication Arts, Cornell University, Ithaca, New York, Bulletin 6.

Cartier, F. A. "Listenability and Human Interest," **Speech Monographs,** 22 (1955), 53.

CRCR Newsletter. Center for Rate Controlled Recordings, University of Louisville, Louisville, Kentucky. Vol. 1–2, 1967, 68.

Deutsch, J. A., and D. Deutsch. "Attention: Some Theoretical Considerations," **Psychological Review,** 70 (1963), 80.

Dickens, Milton, and F. Williams. "An Experimental Application of 'cloze' Procedure and Attitude Measures to Listening Comprehension," **Speech Monographs,** 31 (1964), 103.

Dow, Clyde W. "Listening Instruction at Michigan State: 1954–55," **Journal of Communication,** 5 (1955), 110.

——, and C. E. Irvin. "How We Teach Listening," **Bulletin, National Association of Secondary School Principals,** 38 (1954), 138.

Duker, Sam, and Charles R. Petrie, Jr. "What We Know About Listening: Continuation of a Controversy," **Journal of Communication,** 14 (1964), 245.

"Effective Listening," Xerox Corporation, 1965.

Erickson, A. G. "Can Listening Efficiency Be Improved?" **Journal of Communication,** 4 (1954), 128.

Erway, Ella. "Listening: A Programmed Approach." New York: McGraw-Hill Book Company, 1969.

Fairbanks, Grant, Newman Guttman, and Murray S. Miron. "Auditory Comprehension in Relation to Listening Rate and Selective Verbal Redundancy," **Journal of Speech and Hearing Disorders,** 22 (1957), 23.

——. "Auditory Comprehension of Repeated High-Speech Messages," **Journal of Speech and Hearing Disorders,** 22 (1957), 20.

——. "Effects of Time Compression Upon the Comprehension of Connected Speech," **Journal of Speech and Hearing Disorders,** 22 (1957), 10.

Fessenden, Seth A. "How Can We Teach Listening?" **Journal of Communication,** 2 (1952), 86.

Fillenbaum, Samuel, Lyle V. Jones, and Ammon Rapoport. "The Predictability of Words and Their Grammatical Classes as a Function of Rate of Deletion from a Speech Transcript," **Journal of Verbal Learning and Verbal Behavior,** 2 (1963), 186.

Foulke, Emerson. "The Comprehension of Rapid Speech by the Blind—Part II," Final Progress Report, Performance Research Laboratory, Department of Psychology, Cooperative Research Project No. 1370, University of Louisville, Louisville, Kentucky, 1964.

————, ed. **Proceedings of the Louisville Conference on Time Compressed Speech.** Louisville, Kentucky: Center for Rate Controlled Recordings, 1966.

————. "A Survey of the Acceptability of Rapid Speech," **The New Outlook for the Blind,** November, 1966.

————. "The Comprehension of Rapid Speech by the Blind: Part III," Interim Progress Report, Project No. 2430, Grant No. OE–4–10–127, U.S. Department of Health, Education, and Welfare, 1967.

————. "Listening Comprehension as a Function of Word Rate," **Journal of Communication,** 18 (1968), 198.

————, and Thomas G. Sticht. "Listening Rate Preferences of College Students for Literary Material of Moderate Difficulty," **Journal of Auditory Research,** 6 (1966), 397.

Friedman, Herbert L., David B. Orr, and Cynthia N. Graae. "Further Research on Speeded Speech as an Educational Medium—Materials Comparison Experimentation," Final Report, American Institutes for Research, Silver Spring, Maryland, Grant No. 7–48–7670–267, U.S. Office of Education, 1967.

————, and Raymond L. Johnson. "Compressed Speech: Correlates of Listening Ability," **Journal of Communication,** 18 (1968), 207.

Gerber, Sanford E. "Dichotic and Diotic Presentation of Speeded Speech," **Journal of Communication,** 18 (1968), 272.

Giffin, Kim, and Larry Hannah. "A Study of the Results of an Extremely Short Instrumental Unit in Listening," **Journal of Communication,** 10 (1960), 135.

Goldhaber, G. R., and Carl H. Weaver. "Listener Comprehension of Compressed Speech When the Difficulty, Rate of Presentation, and Sex of the Listener Are Varied," **Speech Monographs,** 35 (1968), 20.

Gore, George V. "A Comparison of Two Methods of Speeded Speech Presented to Blind High School Students," unpublished dissertation, Teachers College, Columbia University.

Gray, Giles Wilkeson, and Claude Merton Wise. **The Bases of Speech.** 3d ed. New York: Harper and Row, 1959.

Hanley, C. N. "A Factorial Analysis of Speech Perception," **Journal of Speech and Hearing Disorders,** 21 (1956), 76.

Heilman, Arthur W. "An Investigation in Measuring and Improving Listening Ability in College Freshmen," **Speech Monographs,** 18 (1951), 302.

Hollingsworth, Paul M. "The Effect of Two Listening Programs on Reading and Listening," **Journal of Communication,** 14 (1964), 19.

———. "Effectiveness of a Course in Listening Improvement for Adults," **Journal of Communication,** 16 (1966), 189.

Hollow, M. K. "Listening Comprehension at the Intermediate Grade Level," **Elementary School Journal,** 56 (1956), 158.

Horowitz, M. W. "Organizational Processes Underlying Differences Between Listening and Reading as a Function of Complexity of Material," **Journal of Communication,** 18 (1968), 37.

———, and Alan Berkowitz. "Listening and Reading, Speaking and Writing: An Experimental Investigation of Differential Acquisition and Reproduction of Memory," **Perceptual and Motor Skills,** 24 (1967), 207.

Irvin, C. E. "Evaluating a Training Program in Listening for College Freshmen," **The School Review,** 61 (1953), 25.

———. "Activities Designed to Improve Listening Skill," **Journal of Communication,** 4 (1954), 14.

Johnson, Kenneth O. "The Effect of Listening Training Upon Listening Comprehension," **Journal of Communication,** 1 (1951), 57.

Johnson, Martha. "The Construction and Analysis of a Listening Test for the Intermediate Grades," unpublished dissertation, Ohio University, 1970.

———, and Don Richardson. "Listening Training in the Fundamentals of Speech Class," **The Speech Teacher,** 17 (1968), 293.

Kelly, Charles M. "An Investigation of the Construct Validity of Two Commercially Published Listening Tests," **Speech Monographs** (1965), 139.

———. "Listening: Complex of Activities—and a Unitary Skill," **Speech Monographs,** 3 (1967), 455.

Kibler, Robert J., Larry L. Barker, and Donald J. Cegala. "Effect of Sex on Comprehension and Retention," **Speech Monographs,** 37 (1970), 287.

Kristofferson, Alfred B. "Attention and Psychophysical Time" in A. Sanders, ed., **Attention and Performance.** Amsterdam: North-Holland, 1967, p. 93.

Leckart, B. T. "Looking Time: The Effects of Stimulus Complexity and Familiarity," **Perception and Psychophysics,** 1 (1966), 142.

———, K. R. Keeling, and P. Bakan. "The Effects of Rate of Presentation on Looking Time," **Perception and Psychophysics,** 1 (1966), 107.

Lewis, N. B. "Listen, Please!" **Clearing House,** 30 (1956), 535.

"Listen and Think," Educational Development Laboratories, 1969.

Loper, James L. "An Experimental Study of Some Effects of Time Compression upon the Comprehension and Retention of a Visually Augmented Televised Speech," **Dissertation Abstracts,** 27 (1967), 4370.

McCracken, Sally. "Comprehension for Immediate Recall of Time-Compressed Speech as a Function of Sex and Level of Activation" in Emerson Foulke, ed., **Proceedings of the Second Louisville Conference on Rate and/or Frequency-Controlled Speech.** Louisville: Center for Rate Controlled Recordings, University of Louisville, 1971, p. 313.

McDonald, Adelbert C. "The Teaching of Listening Skills at the Ninth Grade Level," unpublished thesis, University of Kansas, 1960.

Meyer, John L., and Frederick Williams. "Teaching Listening at the Secondary Level: Some Evaluations," **The Speech Teacher,** 14 (1965), 299.

Moray, N. "Broadbent's Filter Theory: Postulate H and the Problem of Switching Time," **Quarterly Journal of Experimental Psychology,** 12 (1960), 214.

————, and T. Barnett. "Stimulus Presentation and Methods of Scoring in Short-Term Memory Experiments," **Acta Psychologie,** 24 (1965), 253.

Morton, J. "Interaction of Information in Word Recognition," **Psychological Review,** 76 (1969), 165.

Newman, John, and M. W. Horowitz. "Organizational Processes Underlying Differences Between Listening and Reading as a Function of Complexity of Material," paper read at the annual convention of the Speech Association of the Eastern States, 1964.

Nichols, Ralph G. "Factors in Listening Comprehension," **Speech Monographs,** 15 (1948), 154.

————. "Ten Components of Effective Listening." **Journal of the National Association of Elementary School Principals,** 37 (1958), 21.

Niles, Doris. "Teaching Listening in the Fundamentals Course," **The Speech Teacher,** 6 (1957), 300.

Norman, D. A. "Acquisition and Retention in Short-Term Memory," **Journal of Experimental Psychology,** 72 (1966), 369.

————. "Memory While Shadowing," **Quarterly Journal of Experimental Psychology,** 21 (1969), 85.

Orr, David B. "A Note on Thought as a Function of Reading and Listening Rates," **Perceptual and Motor Skills,** 19 (1964), 174.

————. "Time Compressed Speech—a Perspective," **Journal of Communication,** 18 (1968), 288.

————, and Herbert L. Friedman. "The Effect of Listening Aids on the Comprehension of Time-Compressed Speech," **Journal of Communication,** 17 (1967), 223.

Petrie, Charles R., Jr. "The Experimental Evaluation of a Program for the

Improvement of Listening in the Elementary School," **Speech Monographs,** 29 (1962), 94.

—————. "An Experimental Evaluation of Two Methods for Improving Listening Comprehension Abilities," **Speech Monographs,** 29 (1962), 94.

—————. "What We Don't Know About Listening," **Journal of Communication,** 14 (1964), 248.

Pratt, E. "Experimental Evaluation of a Program for the Improvement of Listening," **Elementary School Journal,** 56 (1956), 315.

Reid, Ronald. "Grammatical Complexity and Comprehension of Compressed Speech," **Journal of Communication,** 18 (1968), 236.

Renwick, Ralph, Jr. "A Listening Course for High School Seniors," **The Speech Teacher,** 6 (1957), 59.

Rossiter, Charles M. "The Effects of Rate of Presentation on Listening Test Scores for Recall of Facts, Recall of Ideas, and Generation of Inferences," unpublished dissertation, Ohio University, 1970.

Schmidt, Marianne W., and Alfred B. Kristofferson. "Discrimination of Successiveness: A Test of a Model of Attention," **Science,** 139 (1963), 112.

"Sequential Tests of Educational Progress," Cooperative Test Division, Educational Testing Service, Princeton, New Jersey, 1957.

Shiffrin, R. M., and R. C. Atkinson. "Storage and Retrieval Processes in Long-Term Memory," **Psychological Review,** 76 (1969), 179.

Shriner, Thomas, and Willard Zemlin. **CRCR Newsletter,** Louisville: Center for Rate Controlled Recordings, 1 (1967), 1.

—————, and William Sprague. "Responses of Third-Grade Children to Commands at Varying Rates of Compression," **CRCR Newsletter,** Louisville: Center for Rate Controlled Recordings, 2 (1968), 1.

Sincoff, Michael Z. "The Development and Comprehension of Isolates of Meaning-Capacity and Their Application to Upward Directed Listening in Industry," unpublished thesis, University of Maryland, 1966.

Spearritt, Donald. **Listening Comprehension—A Factorial Analysis.** Melbourne: Australian Council for Educational Research, Series No. 76, 1962.

Sperling, G. "The Information Available in Brief Visual Presentations," **Psychological Monographs,** 74, No. 498 (1960), 11.

Sticht, Thomas G. "Some Relationships of Mental Aptitude, Reading Ability, and Listening Ability Using Normal and Time-Compressed Speech," **Journal of Communication,** 18 (1968), 243.

Sutherland, N. S., and N. J. McIntosh. "Discrimination Learning: Non-Additivity of Cues," **Nature,** 281 (1964), 528.

Trabasso, Tom, and Gordon H. Bower. **Attention in Learning.** New York: John Wiley & Sons, 1968.

Voelker, Francis H. "A Study of the Effectiveness of Teaching Listening to

Eleventh Grade Students at Foley High School," unpublished thesis, St. Cloud State College, 1959.

Weaver, Carl H., and W. L. Strausbaugh. **The Fundamentals of Speech Communication.** New York: American Book Company, 1964.

Weaver, Wendell, and Albert J. Kingston. "A Factor Analysis of Cloze Procedure and Other Measures of Reading and Language Ability," **Journal of Communication,** 13 (1963), 252.

Wood, David. **CRCR Newsletter,** Louisville: Center for Rate Controlled Recordings, 1 (1967), 3.

Woodcock, Richard W., and Charlotte R. Clark. "Comprehension of a Narrative Passage by Elementary School Children as a Function of Listening Rate, Retention Period, and IQ," **Journal of Communication,** 18 (1968), 259.

Index